Hea

C000052066

Headlong T

FAL

a new version by **Rupert Goold** and **Ben Power**
after **Christopher Marlowe**

MEPHISTOPHELES	**Jason Baughan**
CORNELIUS / VEGA / POPE / OLD MAN	**Andrew Bridgemont**
FOSTER	**Gus Brown**
FAUSTUS	**Michael Colgan**
HELENA	**Claire Lams**
JAKE	**Rocky Marshall**
DINOS	**Tam Mutu**
Original Director	**Rupert Goold**
Director	**Steve Marmion**
Designer	**Laura Hopkins**
Lighting Designer	**Malcolm Rippeth**
Composer & Sound Designer	**Adam Cork**
Video & Projection Designer	**Lorna Heavey**
Casting Director	**Janine Snape**
Production Manager	**Sam Paterson**
Company Stage Manager	**Graham Michael**
Deputy Stage Manager	**Helen Bowen**
Assistant Stage Manager	**Bonnie Morris**
Costume Supervisor	**Mia Flodquist**
Wardrobe Mistress	**Beth Howard**
Relighter & Production Electrician	**Clare O'Donoghue**
Resounder	**David Pringle**
Production Assistant	**Jennifer Stowar**
Production Insurance	**Walton & Parkinson Ltd**
Press	**Nicola Conibere**
Production Photography	**Manuel Harlan**
Graphic Design	**Eureka!**

Presented by Headlong Theatre in association with Hampstead Theatre
and Royal & Derngate, Northampton

**This production was first performed at
Nuffield Theatre, Southampton on 18th October 2007**

'This is hell, nor am I out of it'

The idea of freely adapting Christopher Marlowe's *Doctor Faustus* is not a new one. In the 1960s, John Barton adapted and directed a version for the RSC which featured text from various renderings of the Faust legend, interwoven with a reduced version of the Marlowe. The original play is magnificent in its vision, its poetry, its humanity. Yet the text, as in other Marlowe plays, sometimes feels imprecise. Many scenes speak to us with the precision and clarity of dramatic masterpieces, but others are tonally inconsistent. Whether this is an accurate reflection of the original play or the result of 400 years of textual corruption is impossible to say, but it was clear to Rupert Goold and me at the beginning of the adaptation process that some editing was required.

We became committed to boiling the play down and to producing a shortened, tightened version of Marlowe's text. This then left room for us to insert a contemporary plotline which echoed and questioned the original. Our aim was to find a parallel which excavated the Marlowe and raised questions, which challenged an audience rather than instructed them. We wanted to find a modern situation that replicated the controversy, the whiff of danger, that necromancy embodied for Elizabethan playgoers, but that also possessed a heightened quality, a certain poetry, that raised it above the everyday.

It is these qualities that attracted us to the world of modern art and to the Chapman Brothers in particular. It should be noted immediately that the characters of Jake and Dinos in this play, and their journey within it, are fictional. They are inspired by actual people and events but have been heightened, dramatised and at times entirely reinvented to suit our purpose. We've tried to tell a story which is theatrical, modern and metaphorical. A story that examines the irrevocable act, the deed which cannot be undone. In short, we've tried to create a modern companion for Marlowe's play, harness it to the original and then see what connections and collisions occur for an audience.

Ben Power

CAST

JASON BAUGHAN (*Mephistopheles*)

Theatre includes: *Twelfth Night, Taming of the Shrew* (Propeller, Old Vic and Tour); *The Winter's Tale* (Propeller); *Blood Wedding* (Almeida Theatre); *Festen* (Lyric and West End); *Season's Greetings* (Yvonne Arnaud, UK tour); *Love's a Luxury, Clockwatching, Whispers Along the Patio* (Orange Tree/Stephen Joseph); *Peribanez* (Young Vic); *Much Ado About Nothing* (AFTLS); *Measure for Measure, The Tempest, Twelfth Night* (RSC); *Three Sisters, Have You Anything To Declare, A Midsummer Night's Dream* (Orange Tree); *The Dove* (Croydon Warehouse).

Television includes: *Doctors, Inspector Lynley Mysteries, The Bill*.

ANDREW BRIDGMONT
(*Cornelius/Vega/Pope/Old Man*)

Theatre includes: *The Mozart Question* (Bristol Old Vic); *Love and Other Fairytales, Sisters and Others* (Scarlet Theatre Co.); *Life of Galileo, Wilfred* (Birmingham Rep); *Cue Deadly: A Film Live on Stage* (Riverside Studios); *Hard Times, Dangerous Corner* (Watermill Theatre); *An Inspector Calls* (P.W. Productions); *The Winter's Tale, The Maid's Tragedy* (Shakespeare's Globe); *Twelfth Night* (Imaginary Forces); *Casement* (Moving Theatre); *Much Ado About Nothing* (Thelma Holt); *Dracula* (Cannizaro Park); *Measure for Measure* (Maison Berteau); *The Tempest* (Phoebus Cart, Tour); *Cymbeline, Hamlet, A Clockwork Orange* (RSC); *Small Moments* (Royal Festival Hall).

Television includes: *Waking the Dead, Party Animals, Family Man, Riot at the Rite, Hustle, Who Killed Charles Bravo?, EastEnders, Murphy's Law, M.I.T., Single, Casualty, The Bill, History of Warfare, No Bananas, 999, Soldier Soldier, Between the Lines*.

Radio includes: *The Prisoner of Papa Stour*.

GUS BROWN (*Foster*)

Theatre includes: *Jeremy Lion for Your Entertainment* (Menier Chocolate Factory); *Laurence & Gus: Next In Line, Laurence & Gus: Men In Love* (Edinburgh); *A History of the World in Five and a Half Sketches* (Soho Theatre and Edinburgh); *The Blue Diamond of Azkabar* (Changeling Theatre); *The Waves* (Passepartout/BAC); *Eurydice* (Whitehall Theatre); *Design for Living* (ETT and UK Tour).

Television includes: *That Mitchell & Webb Look, Green Wing, Broken News, Tynan – In Praise of Hardcore, The Robinsons, The All New Harry Hill Show, My Hero, Chambers, The Mitchell & Webb Situation, Happiness.*

Radio includes: *Laurence & Gus: Men in Love, Laurence & Gus: Untold Stories, What A Carve Up!, Rigor Mortis.*

MICHAEL COLGAN (*Faustus*)

Theatre includes: *How Much is Your Iron, Bedtime Story & The End of The Beginning, This Lime Tree Bower* (Young Vic); *Hysteria* (Northcott Theatre); *Major Barbara, Playboy of the Western World* (Royal Exchange); *Blue on Blue* (Haymarket Theatre, Basingstoke); *The Cherry Orchard, The Tempest, The Freedom of the City, Amazing Grace* (Abbey Theatre); *Ten Rounds* (Tricycle Theatre); *A Midsummer Night's Dream* (RSC); *Faithful Dealing* (Soho Theatre); *Dolly West's Kitchen* (Old Vic and Abbey Theatre); *Paddy Irishman, Paddy Englishman* (Birmingham Rep); *How I Learned to Drive* (Donmar Warehouse); *The Voyage of the Dawn Trader, Animal Farm* (Lyric Theatre, Belfast); *Ripley Bogle* (Grace Theatre).

Television includes: *Silent Witness, Soundproof, Animals, Chernobyl, The Year London Blew Up, The Long Firm, Wall of Silence, Sinners, Sunday, Rebel Heart.*

Film includes: *This is Not a Love Song, The Eliminator.*

CLAIRE LAMS (*Helena*)

Training: Queen Margaret University College

Theatre includes: *Fabulation* (Tricycle Theatre); *Presence* (Plymouth Theatre); *Harvest* (Royal Court); *Chimps* (Liverpool Playhouse); *Citizenship* (National Theatre Studio); *Fields of Gold*, *Soap* (Stephen Joseph); *Coming Around Again*, *Huddersfield* (West Yorkshire Playhouse); *Happiest Days of Your Life* (Royal Exchange); *The Dice House* (Birmingham); *Romeo and Juliet* (Shakespeare in the Park).

Television includes: *Holby City, Silent Witness, The Brief, The Bill, EastEnders*.

Film includes: *Pumpkinhead, Southwark: The Movie, Cerberus, Praise*.

ROCKY MARSHALL (*Jake*)

Training: Mountview Academy of Theatre Arts

Theatre includes: *Rabbit* (Old Red Lion); *Macbeth* (Wimbledon Theatre); *What About Leonardo* (Lillian Bayliss); *Piaf* (West End and Tour); *Romeo and Juliet* (Oval, Kennington).

Television includes: *The Royal, Rome, Dalziel and Pascoe, Holby City, Band of Brothers, The Affair, The Bill, EastEnders, Doctors, Bostock's Cup, Family Affairs, Bugs, London's Burning, Casualty*.

Film includes: *Mr. Right, Mean Machine, Hart's War, Clancy's Kitchen, Vegas Shift, Ama, Flying Colours*.

TAM MUTU (*Dinos*)

Theatre includes: *The Royal Hunt of the Sun, Love's Labour's Lost, Anything Goes, South Pacific* (RNT); *East* (Leicester Haymarket); *King Lear, Romeo & Juliet* (RSC); *As You Like It, Romeo and Juliet, Oh! What A Lovely War* (Regent's Park); *Les Misérables* (Palace Theatre).

Television includes: *Holby City, Doctors, Footballer's Wives*.

CREATIVE TEAM

Rupert Goold (Original Director/Writer)

Rupert is Artistic Director of Headlong Theatre. Productions for Headlong include *Rough Crossings, Faustus, Restoration* and *Paradise Lost*. From 2002-5 he was Artistic Director of the Royal and Derngate Theatres in Northampton and an Associate Artist at Salisbury Playhouse 1996-97.

Other theatre includes: *Macbeth* (Chichester Theatre/Gielgud); *The Glass Menagerie* (Apollo); *The Tempest, Speaking Like Magpies* (RSC); *Scaramouche Jones* (national and international tours); *Gone to LA, Sunday Father* (Hampstead Theatre); *The Colonel Bird* (Gate); *Hamlet, Othello, Waiting for Godot, Insignificance, The Weir, Betrayal, Arcadia, Summer Lightning* (Royal and Derngate Theatres); *The End of the Affair, Dancing at Lughnasa, Habeus Corpus* (Salisbury Playhouse); *Travels with my Aunt* (Salisbury Playhouse and national tour); *Broken Glass* (Watford Palace); *Privates on Parade* (New Vic); *The Wind in the Willows* (Birmingham Rep).

Opera includes: *Le Comte Ory* (Garsington Opera); *L'Opera Seria, Gli Equivoci, Il Pomo D'Oro* (Batignano).

Ben Power (Writer)

Ben Power is Literary Associate of Headlong Theatre.

His work for the stage includes: *A Disappearing Number* for Complicite (international tour and Barbican); the forthcoming *A Tender Thing* for the Royal Shakespeare Company; *Paradise Lost* (Royal Theatre, Northampton and national tour); *Faustus* (Hampstead Theatre); versions of *The Tempest* and *Much Ado About Nothing* for the RSC Complete Works Festival (Swan Theatre and national tours); *Tamburlaine the Great* (Bankside Rose); and *Julius Caesar* (Menier Chocolate Factory).

He has acted as dramaturg for Headlong, the RSC, Complicite and Shakespeare's Globe. Current projects include *Gulliver's Travels* for Headlong and a new play for the RSC.

Steve Marmion (Director)

Steve is currently Associate Director at the RSC on their new season following a successful year with them on the Complete Works. He works regularly with the National Theatre, RSC and Headlong. He has been a script reader for Act productions, Channel 4, the National Theatre and the Royal Court YWP.

Theatre as Director includes: *A Date to Remember* (Soho Theatre); *Ghetto* (Watford Palace Theatre); *The Sleeping Beauty, Miranda's Mirror, Tiny Tales* (Stephen Joseph Theatre); *Madam Butterfly's Child, Mad Margaret's Revenge* (national tours); *More than Just a Game, SK8, Speak After the Beep, Pinter Shorts, Multiplex* (Theatre Royal Plymouth); *Team Spirit* (National Theatre - Connections); *The Jungle Book, Rhinoceros, The Visit, Big Brother* (Sherman Theatre); *97 - Hillsborough, Caliban's Island, The Club* (Touched Theatre).

Theatre as associate or assistant director includes: Ionesco's *Macbett, Macbeth, The Tempest, Antony and Cleopatra, Julius Caesar* (RSC); *Country Music* (Simon Stephens, Royal Court); *Little Sweet Thing* (Roy Williams, Eclipse Theatre); *24 Hour Plays* (Old Vic); *Edward Gant's Amazing Feats of Loneliness* (Anthony Nielson, Theatre Royal Plymouth).

Awards include: London One Act Theatre Festival - Best Production 2005, Best New Play 2004.

Laura Hopkins (Designer)

Laura trained in interior design and at the Motley Theatre Design Course.

Recent work includes: *Rough Crossings* (Headlong); *Stockholm* (Frantic Assembly); *The Class Club* (Duckie); *Black Watch* (National Theatre Scotland); costumes on *Sinatra!* (London Palladium); *Mercury Fur* (Paines Plough); *The Three Musketeers* (Bristol Old Vic); *Hotel Methuselah* (Imitating the Dog); *The Escapologist* (Suspect Culture); *Mister Heracles* (TMA winner, Best Design; West Yorkshire Playhouse); *The Golden Ass, Macbeth* (Shakespeare's Globe); *Così Fan Tutte, Falstaff* (English National Opera); *Hamlet, Faustus* (TMA winner, Best Design), and *Othello* (also nominated for the TMA Award; Northampton Royal); *Elixir of Love* (New Zealand Opera); *Swan Lake Re-mixed* (Vienna Volksoper); *Carnesky's Ghost Train* (a visual theatre ride) and the *International Necronautical Society Broadcasting Unit* (ICA).

She is currently working on *Peer Gynt* for the Guthrie Theatre, Minneapolis, *The Merchant of Venice* at the RSC and *Kellerman* with Imitating the Dog.

Malcolm Rippeth (Lighting Designer)

Malcolm lit *Faustus* for Headlong at Hampstead. Other theatre includes: *Brief Encounter* (Kneehigh/Birmingham Rep); *Tutti Frutti* (National Theatre of Scotland); *Cymbeline* (Kneehigh/RSC); *Nights at the Circus* (Kneehigh/Lyric Hammersmith); *The Bacchae* (Kneehigh); *Starseeker* (Royal Theatre Northampton); *Cyrano de Bergerac* (Bristol Old Vic); *Hamlet* (ETT/West End); *Mother Courage, Romeo and Juliet* (ETT); *Scuffer, The Lion, the Witch and the Wardrobe, Homage to Catalonia* (West Yorkshire Playhouse); *Mrs Warren's Profession* (Edinburgh Lyceum); *Trance* (Bush); *The Little Prince, Great Expectations, Kaput!, The Snow Queen* (Northern Stage); *Monkey* (Dundee Rep); *Hay Fever, Macbeth* (York Theatre Royal); *Lush Life, Toast* (Live Theatre); *Coelacanth, Black Cocktail* (Pleasance Edinburgh); *Dealer's Choice* (Salisbury); *Antigone at Hell's Mouth* (NYT); *Keepers of the Flame* (RSC/Live Theatre) and forthcoming *Beauty and the Beast* (West Yorkshire Playhouse).

Other work includes: *Carmen Jones* (Royal Festival Hall); *Seven Deadly Sins* (WNO/Diversions Dance); *The Ball, La Vie des Fantasmes Érotiques et Esthétiques, La Nuit Intime* and *Angelmoth* (balletLORENT) and *The Philosophers' Stone* (Garsington Opera).

Adam Cork (Composer & Sound Designer)

Adam read music at Cambridge University, studying composition with Robin Holloway.

Theatre includes: Scores and sound designs for *Frost/Nixon* (Donmar/Gielgud/Broadway); *Suddenly Last Summer* (Albery); *Don Carlos, Macbeth* (Gielgud); *The Glass Menagerie* (Apollo); *Speaking Like Magpies* (RSC Swan); *The Tempest* (RSC RST/Michigan/Novello); *Caligula, The Wild Duck, Don Juan in Soho, John Gabriel Borkman* (Donmar Warehouse); *The Late Henry Moss, Tom and Viv* (Almeida); *On the Third Day* (New Ambassadors, subject of Channel 4 documentary *The Play's the Thing*); *Underneath the Lintel* (Duchess); *On the Ceiling* (Garrick); *Scaramouche Jones* (Riverside Studios/World Tour); *Troilus and Cressida* (Old Vic); *Rough Crossings, Faustus, Restoration, Paradise Lost* (Headlong); *Nine Parts of Desire* (Wilma Theatre Philadelphia); *Lear, The Cherry Orchard* (Sheffield Crucible); *Romeo and Juliet* (Manchester Royal Exchange); *The Government Inspector* (Chichester Festival); *Macbeth* (Chichester Minerva); *My Uncle Arly* (Royal Opera House Linbury); *The Field* (Tricycle); winner of the TMA Award for Best Show for Young People, *Alice's Adventures in Wonderland* (Bristol Old Vic).

Film and television includes: *Frances Tuesday, Re-ignited, Imprints, Bust, The Three Rules of Infidelity, Sexdrive, Tripletake*.

Radio includes: *Losing Rosalind, The Luneberg Variation, The Colonel-Bird, Don Carlos*.

Adam was nominated for the 2005 Olivier Award for Best Sound Design for *Suddenly Last Summer* (Albery). He also received a 2007 Outstanding Music for a Play Drama Desk Award nomination, for the Broadway production of *Frost/Nixon*.

Lorna Heavey (Video & Projection Designer)

Lorna is a multi-disciplinary artist and filmmaker. She trained in Fine Art at Düsseldorf Art Academy (Nam June Paik & Nan Hoover), Kingston University, Chelsea School of Art. She is founder of Headfirst Foundation, a cross platform artists collective, and elected Fellow of The Royal Society of Arts.

Video design credits include: *Macbeth* (West End & Minerva, Chichester); *I Am Shakespeare* (Minerva, Chichester); *The Caucasian Chalk Circle* (National Theatre); *The Tempest* (RSC West End); *Speaking Like Magpies* (RSC Swan); *Phaedra* (Donmar); *Vanishing Point, Genoa 01* (Complicite, Royal Court); *Rough Crossings, Faustus, Paradise Lost* (Headlong); *Cooped* (Purcell Rooms and international tour); *Tall Phoenix* (Belgrade); *Betrayal* (Northampton); *Cleansed* (Arcola); *I Am Thicker Than Water* (This Way Up Tour); *The Waves* (BAC); *Mahabharata* (Sadler's Wells); *Dido And Aeneas* (Opera North); *Very Opera* (Cologne). Set design includes: *Hamlet Machine* (KunstHalle Berlin/BAC); *Trajectory* (European tour); *Titus Andronicus* (BAC); *A Stitch in Time, Beautiful Beginnings* (Theatre 503). Writing and directing credits for theatre and film include: *A Stitch in Time, Beautiful Beginnings, Several Words* (Split/Hanover Film Festival); *Timed Existence* (Edinburgh Film Festival); *The Global Conditioned, Duet for One Voice* (Film Festival, Berlin).

Art Exhibitions include shows at ICA, RIBA, Dada Dandies Berlin, Poznan Poland, Budapest Academy, Roppongi Tokyo.

Television includes: *The Mighty Boosh* (BBC), *The Bendix Report* (C4).

Acknowledgements

Associate Directors: Fran Morley, Kate Sorahan, Gemma Nicol, Adam Forde

With thanks to: Charlie Payne, Reena Lalbihari, Kate Padbury, Matthew Vere, Andy Bainbridge, Lee Griffiths, Greta Clough, Verity Woolnough, Isabelle & Elinor Agerbak, Miranda Colchester, LAMDA, Claudio Von Planta, Karzan Sherabayani, Optical Marketplace, Hampstead Theatre

Headlong

HEADLONG: /hedl'ong/ *noun* 1. with head first,
2. starting boldly, 3. to approach with speed and vigour

Headlong Theatre is dedicated to new ways of making theatre.
By exploring revolutionary writers and practitioners of the past
and commissioning new work from artists from a wide variety of
backgrounds we aim constantly to push the imaginative
boundaries of the stage. **Headlong** makes exhilarating,
provocative and spectacular new work to take around the country
and around the world.

Coming soon from Headlong

THE LAST DAYS OF JUDAS ISCARIOT
by Stephen Adly Guirgis directed by Rupert Goold

THE ENGLISH GAME
by Richard Bean directed by Sean Holmes

*'Headlong's first season is a mouthwatering
array of major works'* **Telegraph**

'One of our most exciting and flamboyant directors'
Time Out on Rupert Goold

Artistic Director	**Rupert Goold**
Executive Producer	**Henny Finch**
Finance Manager	**Julie Renwick**
Literary Associate	**Ben Power**
Assistant Producer	**Jenni Kershaw**

**For more information or to join our mailing list, please go to
www.headlongtheatre.co.uk**

FAUSTUS

Rupert Goold and Ben Power

after Christopher Marlowe

Faustus was first performed at the Royal Theatre, Northampton, on 24 October 2004, and subsequently at Hampstead Theatre, London, in 2006.

Director   Rupert Goold
Designer   Laura Hopkins
Lighting Designer   Rick Fisher/Malcolm Rippeth
Composer and Sound Designer   Adam Cork

Characters
in order of appearance

FAUSTUS
GOOD ANGEL
EVIL ANGEL
CORNELIUS
MATTHEW FOSTER, *an art critic*
HELENA, *a camera technician*
JAKE CHAPMAN, *an artist*
DINOS CHAPMAN, *his brother, an artist*
MEPHISTOPHELES
POLICEMAN, *voice on the phone*
VEGA, *a Spanish art dealer*
LUCIFER
POPE
FIRST FRIAR
SECOND FRIAR
OLD MAN
MINTA
ART DEALER
SPACED-OUT DRUGGY
DRUNK STUDENT
FEMALE JOURNALIST

Also
CROWD *at the Turner Prize ceremony*
Party of FRIARS

This text went to press before the end of rehearsals and may differ slightly from the play as performed.

ACT ONE

Scene One – The Doctor

A small medieval room, lined with books. FAUSTUS *revealed.*

FAUSTUS. Settle thy studies, Faustus, and begin
    To sound the depth of that thou wilt profess:
    Having commenc'd, be a divine in show,
    Yet level at the end of every art,
    And live and die in Aristotle's works.
    Sweet *Analytics*, 'tis thou hast ravish'd me!
    'Bene disserere est finis logices.'
    Is to dispute well logic's chiefest end?
    Affords this art no greater miracle?
    Then read no more; thou hast attain'd that end:
    A greater subject fitteth Faustus' wit:
    Be a physician, Faustus; heap up gold,
    And be eterniz'd for some wondrous cure:
    'Summum bonum medicinae sanitas',
    The end of physic is our body's health.
    Why, Faustus, hast thou not attain'd that end?
    Is not thy common talk found aphorisms?
    Are not thy bills hung up as monuments,
    Whereby whole cities have escap'd the plague,
    And thousand desperate maladies been eas'd?
    Yet art thou still but Faustus, and a man.
    Couldst thou make men to live eternally,
    Or, being dead, raise them to life again,
    Then this profession were to be esteem'd.
    Physic, farewell! Where is Justinian?
    'Si una eademque res legatur duobus, alter rem, alter
        valorem rei, &c.'
    A pretty case of paltry legacies!
    Such is the subject of the institute,
    And universal body of the law:

This study fits a mercenary drudge,
Who aims at nothing but external trash;
Too servile and illiberal for me.
When all is done, divinity is best:
Jerome's Bible, Faustus; view it well.
'Stipendium peccati mors est. Ha! Stipendium, &c.'
The reward of sin is death: that's hard.
'If we say that we have no sin, we deceive ourselves, and
*   there's no truth in us. Why, then, belike we must sin, and*
*   so consequently die.'*
Ay, we must die an everlasting death.
What doctrine call you this, *Che sera, sera,*
What will be, shall be? Divinity, adieu!
These metaphysics of magicians,
And necromantic books are heavenly;
Lines, circles, scenes, letters, and characters;
Ay, these are those that Faustus most desires.
O, what a world of profit and delight,
Of power, of honour, of omnipotence,
Is promis'd to the studious artizan!
All things that move between the quiet poles
Shall be at my command: emperors and kings
Are but obeyed in their several provinces,
Nor can they raise the wind, or rend the clouds;
But his dominion that exceeds in this,
Stretcheth as far as doth the mind of man;
A sound magician is a mighty god:
Here, Faustus, tire thy brains to gain a deity.
I've sent word to my friend Cornelius,
Requesting him today to visit me.
His conference will be a greater help to me
Than all my labours, plod I ne'er so fast.

Enter GOOD ANGEL *and* EVIL ANGEL.

GOOD ANGEL. O, Faustus, lay that damnèd book aside,
    And gaze not on it, lest it tempt thy soul,
    And heap God's heavy wrath upon thy head!
    Read, read the Scriptures: that is blasphemy.

EVIL ANGEL. Go forward, Faustus, in that famous art
   Wherein all Nature's treasure is contain'd:
   Be thou on earth as Jove is in the sky,
   Lord and commander of these elements.

Exit ANGELS.

FAUSTUS. How am I glutted with conceit of this!
   Shall I make spirits fetch me what I please,
   Resolve me of all ambiguities,
   Perform what desperate enterprise I will?
   I'll have them fly to India for gold,
   Ransack the ocean for orient pearl,
   And search all corners of the new-found world
   For pleasant fruits and princely delicates;
   I'll have them read me strange philosophy,
   And tell the secrets of all foreign kings;
   I'll have them wall all Germany with brass,
   And make swift Rhine circle fair Wertenberg;
   I'll have them fill the public schools with silk,
   Wherewith the students shall be bravely clad;
   I'll levy soldiers with the coin they bring,
   And reign sole king of all the provinces;
   Yea, stranger engines for the brunt of war,
   Than was the fiery keel at Antwerp's bridge,
   I'll make my servile spirits to invent.

A knock on the door. Enter CORNELIUS.

Come enter here, German Cornelius,
And make me blest with your sage conference.
Know that your words have won me at the last
To practise magic and concealèd arts:
Yet not your words only, but mine own fantasy,
That will receive no object; for my head
But ruminates on necromantic skill.
Philosophy is odious and obscure;
Both law and physic are for petty wits;
Divinity is basest of the three,
Unpleasant, harsh, contemptible, and vile:

'Tis magic, magic, that hath ravish'd me.
Then, gentle friend, aid me in this attempt;
And I, that have with concise syllogisms
Gravell'd the pastors of the German church,
And made the flowering pride of Wertenberg
Swarm to my problems, as the infernal spirits
On sweet Musaeus when he came to hell,
Will be as cunning as Agrippa was,
Whose shadow made all Europe honour him.

CORNELIUS. Faustus, these books, thy wit, and my
        experience,
Shall make all nations to canonise us.
As Indian Moors obey their Spanish lords,
So shall the spirits of every element
Be always serviceable to us two;
Like lions shall they guard us when we please;
Like Almain rutters with their horsemen's staves,
Or Lapland giants, trotting by our sides;
Sometimes like women, or unwedded maids,
Shadowing more beauty in their airy brows
Than have the white breasts of the queen of love:
If learnèd Faustus will be resolute.

FAUSTUS. My friend as resolute am I in this
    As thou to live: therefore object it not.

CORNELIUS. The miracles that magic will perform
    Will make thee vow to study nothing else.
    He that is grounded in astrology,
    Enrich'd with tongues, well seen in minerals,
    Hath all the principles magic doth require:
    Then doubt not, Faustus, but to be renowm'd,
    And more frequented for this mystery
    Than heretofore the Delphian oracle.
    The spirits tell me they can dry the sea,
    And fetch the treasure of all foreign wrecks,
    Ay, all the wealth that our forefathers hid
    Within the massy entrails of the earth:
    Then tell me, Faustus, what shall we two want?

FAUSTUS. Nothing, Cornelius. O, this cheers my soul!
    Come, show me some demonstrations magical,
    That I may conjure in some lusty grove,
    And have these joys in full possession.

CORNELIUS. Then haste thee to some solitary grove,
    And bear wise Bacon's and Albertus' works,
    The Hebrew Psalter, and New Testament;
    And whatsoever else is requisite
    I will inform thee ere our conference cease.
    First I shall let thee know the words of art;
    And then, all other ceremonies learn'd,
    Faustus may try his cunning by himself.
    When I've instructed thee the rudiments,
    And then wilt thou be perfecter than I.

FAUSTUS. Then come and dine with me, and, after meat,
    We'll canvass every quiddity thereof;
    For, ere I sleep, I'll try what I can do:
    This night I'll conjure, though I die therefore.

    Exeunt.

Scene Two – An Announcement

The studio of the CHAPMAN BROTHERS. *Two people appear to be waiting,* FOSTER, *an art critic, and* HELENA, *a camera technician of Middle-Eastern extraction.* HELENA *unpacks her camera and sound equipment.* FOSTER *breezes about the studio.*

HELENA (*holding a personal mic out to* FOSTER). May I . . . ?

FOSTER. Oh yes, of course.

    She spools it under his shirt. He seems slightly irritated.

    Where's Minta?

HELENA. I'm sorry?

FOSTER. Minta? I did ask Pablo for Minta. It's not as if this isn't important.

HELENA. I start just today. From features.

FOSTER. Typical. Once again the BBC excels itself . . . I'm sure you're very good, it's just, well, usually Minta films my pieces . . .

HELENA looks confused. Beat.

You are ready to film at once?

HELENA. Yes . . . I must . . . (*She holds up her personal mics.*) . . . for sound.

FOSTER. Yes, yes, I know. It's just we won't have long and, as Pablo clearly fails to realise, this could be a scoop of monumental proportions.

Silence. The sound of music from a car passing outside. HELENA picks up a toy soldier.

HELENA. He is a toymaker?

FOSTER (*snorting*). No, he's not a toymaker. They are artists.

FOSTER checks watch and smoothes his hair. Pause.

HELENA (*looking around the studio uncertainly*). Artists?

FOSTER. Yes. Didn't anyone tell you before you came out?

HELENA. No. This is my first time for BBC4. There was problem today – other cameras busy.

FOSTER. I see. (*Sighs.*) Listen, I'm sorry to be tetchy – it's just that these two are notoriously secretive and they don't often give interviews about their work. Especially before it's even been made.

HELENA. Is strange work.

FOSTER. Strange and wonderful.

HELENA. How, please?

FOSTER. Have you really never heard of the Chapman
    Brothers?

HELENA. No.

FOSTER. Well . . . well . . . that soldier in your hand, that one
    little soldier, let me tell you, was just the beginning. The
    Chapman Brothers made an installation that consisted of a
    series of large perspex cases, about so big, configured as a
    swastika and containing over five thousand hand-moulded
    toy soldiers like that one! They were painted in Nazi outfits
    and were engaged in an endless cycle of extreme brutality
    and Holocaust-like degradation. An Airfix Dachau. They say
    it took them over two years to make.

    Pause.

HELENA (*quietly*). Five thousand Nazi soldiers . . .

FOSTER. And they called it *Hell*. Very Chapmans!

    JAKE CHAPMAN *enters, followed by his brother* DINOS.
    They exude an almost menacing confidence.

JAKE (*nodding to* FOSTER). Matt.

FOSTER (*pleased*). Jake! (*To* DINOS.) Dinos.

DINOS. Matthew.

JAKE. How are you?

FOSTER. I'm great. How are you?

HELENA. May I . . . ?

    HELENA *begins to wire up the* BROTHERS.

FOSTER. Listen, thanks so much for the tip-off. Obviously this
    is a *Late Review* piece but I have a leetle feeling that when
    word gets out this will be a bit more Huw Edwards than
    Mark Lawson!

JAKE. The studio's a bit of a mess . . .

FOSTER. 'The Artist's Cathedral.'

DINOS. What?

FOSTER. Warhol called his studio a 'Cathedral'.

DINOS. . . . Right.

FOSTER. Of course he was having a poke at how little religion
    actually meant to his art, etcetera, etcetera.

JAKE. We ready?

FOSTER. Sorry, yes. Are we rolling? Okay.

HELENA *gives a nod from behind the camera.* FOSTER
takes a set of A3 cards from his bag and goes into presenta-
tion mode.

And . . . 3 – 2 – 1 –

So here I am at the studio of Britart's very own deadly duo –
the Chapman Brothers. The Chapmans have always been at
the hardcore end of the art world. They burst onto the scene
in the early nineties, along with Tracey Emin and Damien
Hirst but if anything they are even more provocative. Their
art can make people feel really uncomfortable – they once
made a set of sculptures of young children with genitals
where they should have faces – but you always sense they
have been building up to something in their work, as though
everything so far has been in anticipation of a piece truly
sensational in every sense. Now they've invited me around
for an exclusive insight into their latest assault on the
modern art scene. What can it be?

He brings the cards into view.

Well, eight years ago in the spring of 1998 the Brothers
caused quite a bit of fuss when they picked up the complete
set of Francisco Goya's etchings *The Disasters of War*.
Though no details of the sale were ever released, reports sug-
gested a six-figure sum. What were these pictures and could
they really be so valuable? Well, in 1810 Napoleon's army
invaded Spain, raping and torturing and being generally

warlike and nasty. Goya, who many people see as the father of modern art, was pretty upset about this and made his set of drawings known as *The Disasters of War*. Most people know Goya for his famous picture *The Executions of the Third of May* from the same period.

He holds up a card with this image.

The Disasters of War are more brutal still, depicting scenes of great suffering in line drawings full of Goya's innate compassion and sense of composition.

He scrolls through cards with the drawings, discarding them one at a time, like Bob Dylan in the 'Subterranean Homesick Blues' video.

They have been called the most revered set of prints in existence and as these reproductions show they're quite, quite ... beautiful. Now they're in the hands of Jake and Dinos Chapman. Crikey! So, guys, where are they now?

JAKE. In a drawer upstairs.

DINOS. Away from sunlight.

FOSTER. And what on earth is the plan?

JAKE. We're painting over them.

DINOS. Tomorrow night.

FOSTER (*to camera gleefully*). So you're actually going to paint over them? Wow ...

DINOS. Tomorrow night.

FOSTER *makes a show of ripping up the cards with the etchings on.*

FOSTER. So, guys, who are you to better Goya?

JAKE. Not better, change. The Goya will be gone ...

DINOS. But something new'll be in its place.

FOSTER. But clearly people will say this is attention-seeking vandalism. Typical of a contemporary art scene in this

country that behaves like The Sex Pistols in the face of the
high Mozartian traditions of fine art. How d'you plead?

JAKE. Give me The Sex Pistols over Mozart any day.

DINOS *sniggers quietly.*

FOSTER. Okay. But obviously a lot of art lovers are going to be
very, very, angry.

JAKE. This country's terrified. Terrified of change. Sometimes
you have to destroy to make.

FOSTER. How d'you mean?

JAKE. Take St Paul's Cathedral. For centuries it's considered
the finest Gothic church in the country.

DINOS. Then along comes Christopher Wren, razes the entire
thing to the ground, and replaces it with his famous inverted
tit. At the time, churchmen claimed he would burn in hell.

JAKE. Look at him now.

FOSTER. Right, but people will say this is just a cheap publicity
stunt proving how lazy and destructive modern artists are.

JAKE. Listen – we don't give a fuck about . . .

FOSTER *mimes a cut and nods to* HELENA.

FOSTER. Ah! We'll have to go again – no swearing before the
watershed . . .

Mimes 3 – 2 – 1 –

But people will say it's a shameless, media-hungry, publicity
stunt.

JAKE (*more considered but with passion*). We, that is my
brother and I, have no interest whatsoever in our celebrity.
Art's not about sensation, it's about commitment. If it draws
attention to itself it's because of its courage, its unflinching
engagement with the world around it, not because it seeks
that attention.

FOSTER. But is this courageous, I wonder?

DINOS. How would you know?

FOSTER. Well, I . . .

DINOS. You're a critic, with due respect, Matt, what on earth could you know about courage?

FOSTER. I suppose . . .

JAKE. Let me tell you about courage, Matthew. Courage is all that matters in art. Most people just don't have the guts to be artists. They have the dreams, sure . . . 'Oh yeah, I wanna be an artist, man' . . . But they don't want to risk giving up on all the million little things in their lives that stop them confronting the world: their cars and kids and final salary pension plans. And so the dreams are strangled and quietly buried for fear they become nightmares.

DINOS. It's all about balls. You've either got them or you haven't. Because sometimes the courageous act has to be the destructive one.

FOSTER. Really?

DINOS. Yeah. Van Gogh didn't cut off his ear to have people talk about him. He did it because he had to. As an artist.

FOSTER. You're hardly cutting off your ear though . . .

DINOS. We're doing something worse.

JAKE. Not self-harm, which people squeal at in delight, but cultural harm.

DINOS. We're doing it because we have to.

FOSTER. Why?

JAKE. Art has lost its power to shock and if art can't shock any more then it loses the very thing that makes it important.

DINOS. Without shock, art becomes just decoration. A distraction. Like the flowers on a grave.

FOSTER. But a lot of people like just looking, taking pleasure from art, from . . .

DINOS. Pretty flowers?

FOSTER. If you like.

DINOS. Then those people are just grazing sheep, obliviously awaiting the abattoir.

FOSTER. Sheep?

DINOS. Yes. But don't worry about them. Help is at hand.

JAKE. We're here! To turn our fellow men from dumb animals into suffering gods.

FOSTER. Is that what you're trying to do?

DINOS. We're doing exactly what Goya did.

FOSTER. Which was?

DINOS. Turn you on.

Beat.

In a dirty way.

Pause.

JAKE. Goya's work fetishises violence.

FOSTER. Fetishises?

JAKE. Yes. Look at these images. They're horrible: murder, rape, castration, but they're also fascinating. Goya didn't show us that war is ugly, pain is ugly, we knew that. He showed us that it's also beguiling, tempting.

DINOS. Pornographic.

FOSTER. You find these images pornographic?

JAKE. Of course they are. Violence is always hypnotic and violence like this is positively addictive. Goya knew that – he's made the first snuff art.

FOSTER. But if you admire these works then why on earth are you destroying them?

JAKE. Because we want to. Because we dare to.

DINOS. And because we can.

JAKE and DINOS *look at each other.*

We've had the series sitting around for a couple of years, every so often taking it out and having a look at it, until we were quite sure that we were ready to rectify the pictures.

FOSTER. You say 'rectify' . . .

JAKE. Yes, it's our term –

FOSTER. Is that Jeff Koons?

DINOS. – from *The Shining.* You remember the scene, Matthew. It's at the bar and the butler's trying to persuade Jack Nicholson to murder his young family – he asks him to 'rectify' the situation.

FOSTER. I see.

JAKE. We will rectify these pictures and so produce a new work of art entirely.

FOSTER. Not so much a 'cover' of Goya as a 'remix'. The art world's Fatboy Slim?

DINOS. If you like.

FOSTER. So will this be an act of painting or performance?

JAKE. Oh, we'll be painting.

FOSTER (*excited*). Really?

DINOS. We're painting over all the faces in the etchings . . . with puppies.

A pause. JAKE *is a little annoyed* DINOS *has let this out.*

FOSTER. Ha-ha.

Beat. He realises they are serious.

Puppies?

DINOS. And clowns.

FOSTER. Puppies and clowns?

JAKE. Yes.

FOSTER. Why?

JAKE. We like puppies.

DINOS. And clowns.

JAKE. And we like clowns.

FOSTER (*not quite sure how to take this*). But . . . err . . . but these pieces are priceless . . .

JAKE. Not priceless, Matthew – we should know.

FOSTER. Fine, but if you're just 'remixing' or 'rectifying' or whatever with puppies and clowns couldn't you just 'rectify' a copy and keep the Goya preserved.

DINOS. No.

JAKE. Then nothing is at stake. Nothing 'happens'.

FOSTER. This isn't some art-school act of youthful provocation, we're talking about Goya! One of the most loved, respected artists of all time.

DINOS. Goya is immaterial! At the end of the day there's only the artwork and the spectator. The artist and the circumstances of the artwork's creation are irrelevant to how it is received.

JAKE. It is the spectator that speaks to the artwork not the other way round. Peter Pan means one thing to a parent and another to a paedophile.

Beat.

If the spectator wants to paint over, wank over, or just plain ignore these pictures then so be it. Democracy in action.

FOSTER. Huh. Democracy . . . or desecration? Rather than recreate the images for yourselves, you're instead destroying Goya's. Were I in the business of psychoanalysis I might say you were jealous.

An edgy moment.

DINOS. Everyone should be jealous of Goya.

FOSTER. Do you think you really understand these works though? Understand them enough to be responsible for their, er, 'rectification'?

DINOS. What?

FOSTER. Well, in doing this, presumably you're claiming that you comprehend these masterpieces as completely, or even more completely, than Goya himself did. Arrogance?

JAKE. If you're implying that we lack a sufficient appreciation of Goya, which I think you are . . .

FOSTER. I'm not but oth . . .

JAKE (*overlapping*). . . . then you show complete ignorance, Matt. Ignorance about us, about our work and about how central Goya has always been to it. We understand these pieces. Whatever the fuck that means! Not in the same way Goya did. In a different, incomparable way. Filtered through two hundred years of perspective and through our own vision as artists. It's this unique appreciation that led us to acquire these works at considerable personal expense.

DINOS. It is this appreciation that allows us, and us alone, to make this act tomorrow night.

JAKE. That's not arrogance. That's self-belief.

FOSTER. But imagine if some artist in the future decided to 'rectify' one of your pieces. How would you feel then?

JAKE. Matt. This isn't about tit for tat and it's certainly not about how we feel. Feeling doesn't come into it – art isn't about the artist's feelings. The job of a work of art is to raise questions about its terms and conditions and how it was made. That's what we do. We present the viewer with a puzzle. We put a stop to speedy consumption. We refuse to offer a straightforward aesthetic experience. And to defend the integrity of the work, we produce a bit of turbulence that makes it more than a simple sip – of art . . .

FOSTER. Turbulence . . .

They are in full fly but HELENA *quietly interrupts to fix* JAKE*'s mic.*

HELENA. Sorry.

JAKE. That's fine. Where was I?

DINOS. Turbulence. Feelings.

JAKE (*firmly*). Oh yeah. This new piece has been two years in development. We've had many 'feelings' in that time but the integrity we represent tomorrow night has nothing to do with anything as bourgeois as feeling or worse still of 'beauty'. Tomorrow night we are making art that will cause reaction not reflection. Tomorrow night we're changing the world and the world will sit up and notice.

DINOS. They'll notice because we'll do something, create something that gets under the skin so deep that you feel your marrow squirm.

JAKE. Alright, that's your lot!

FOSTER (*to camera*). Well, there you have it, folks. The end of one great work of art tomorrow and maybe – just maybe – the start of another. I'm Matthew Foster and these, as if you needed telling, are the Chapman Brothers. Join us next week when the boys will be stone cladding the Sistine Chapel.

He holds his grin for a moment and HELENA *lowers the camera.*

(*Unmicing himself.*) Nice one. Quite lively even – ooh, what's that smell? Do I sense the rich aroma of controversy. Ha-ha.

To HELENA.

Can we just get a few pick-ups?

To DINOS.

Can you just talk to me?

DINOS. What about?

FOSTER. Doesn't matter, we just need a few noddy shots. First pet?

FOSTER reacts inappropriately to story.

DINOS. Well, our first pet was a small python that Jake used to put down my trousers. Neither of . . .

FOSTER. Okay, okay, that's great. Thanks.

He turns his phone on which immediately bleeps. JAKE *watches* HELENA *begin packing up and* DINOS *goes over to a TV and turns the sound up a little. He begins to eat a banana.*

Sorry, boys, but I have to make a quick call to 'the office'.

He is already dialling and as he reaches the door . . .

Pablo, Pablo, we have a simply amazing feature on the Chapmans here! . . . You have no idea – it's Duchamps' *Urinal* all over again . . . .

He has left. A long silence. DINOS *absorbed in film.* JAKE *is lost in thought.* HELENA *waiting awkwardly looks at the cards on the floor.*

HELENA. This is them?

JAKE. What?

HELENA. This is the pictures?

JAKE. Oh right. Yeah. Well, those are copies but yeah, that's the Goya.

Pause.

HELENA (*to herself*). There is many suffering here.

JAKE. Do you mean 'much suffering'?

HELENA. Many, many, suffering.

JAKE. Many people?

HELENA. Yes. Both . . . Is war.

JAKE (*unclear*). Yes, it's, it's from a war.

Pause.

What you shooting on?

HELENA *doesn't understand.*

Your camera.

HELENA. Is DV.

JAKE. Is it yours?

HELENA. Yes. I photographer.

JAKE. Where you from?

HELENA. I live in Crystal Palace.

JAKE. Like a princess.

HELENA. I do not understand you.

JAKE. How come you're filming? The camera?

HELENA. I start today. From features.

JAKE. So can you use that thing?

HELENA. Yes. I study Media in Croydon College.

JAKE. What do you make of Croydon, then?

HELENA. Is better than Kabul.

JAKE. I imagine it is.

Beat.

Look, what are you doing tomorrow?

HELENA. Tomorrow?

JAKE. Tomorrow night.

HELENA. Nothing. I think.

JAKE. Come here. Document the evening for us.

HELENA. Document.

JAKE. Yes, we need someone to witness what we're doing, to film it for us – we'll be painting.

HELENA. Here?

JAKE. Yes.

HELENA. Me?

JAKE. Absolutely. We'll pay you – and it'll be fun.

DINOS (*smiling a little unsettlingly*). We're having a party.

HELENA. Okay . . . I will come.

JAKE. Good. Come for nine and bring the camera.

FOSTER bustles back in.

FOSTER. Sorry, sorry, sorry. So look, thanks guys, it's been great. I think it sounds jolly exciting. I mean, let's face it, the kids have no idea who Goya is any more anyway.

Shaking the BROTHERS*' hands.*

Do keep me involved now I've been 'in from the beginning'. For now, I'd better get back to the 'word-piano' . . . Ready to roll?

He makes to leave, followed by HELENA.

DINOS. Hey, what's your name?

FOSTER. Me? My?

HELENA. Helena. My name is Helena.

She leaves. FOSTER *winks at* DINOS.

FOSTER. You devil.

He exits. The BROTHERS *turn to look at each other.*

Scene Three – Conjuring

Enter FAUSTUS *to conjure.*

FAUSTUS. Now that the gloomy shadow of the earth,
  Longing to view Orion's drizzling look,
  Leaps from th' Antarctic world unto the sky,
  And dims the welkin with her pitchy breath,
  Faustus, begin thine incantations,
  And try if devils will obey thy hest,
  Seeing thou hast pray'd and sacrific'd to them.
  Within this circle is Jehovah's name,
  Forward and backward anagrammatiz'd,
  Th' abbreviated names of holy saints,
  Figures of every adjunct to the heavens,
  And characters of signs and erring stars,
  By which the spirits are enforc'd to rise:
  Then fear not, Faustus, but be resolute,
  And try the uttermost magic can perform.
  Sint mihi dei Acherontis propitii! Valeat numen triplex
    Jehovoe! Ignei, aerii, aquatani spiritus, salvete! Orientis
    princeps Belzebub, inferni ardentis monarcha, et
    Demogorgon, propitiamus vos, ut appareat et surgat
    Mephistopheles, quod tumeraris: per Jehovam,
    Gehennam, et consecratam aquam quam nunc spargo,
    signumque crucis quod nunc facio, et per vota nostra,
    ipse nunc surgat nobis dicatus Mephistopheles!

Enter MEPHISTOPHELES.

MEPHISTOPHELES. Now, Faustus, what wouldst thou have
  me do?

FAUSTUS. I charge thee wait upon me whilst I live,
  To do whatever Faustus shall command,
  Be it to make the moon drop from her sphere,
  Or the ocean to overwhelm the world.

MEPHISTOPHELES. I am a servant to great Lucifer,
  And may not follow thee without his leave:
  No more than he commands must we perform.

FAUSTUS. Did not he charge thee to appear to me?

MEPHISTOPHELES. No, I came hither of mine own accord.

FAUSTUS. Did not my conjuring speeches raise thee? Speak.

MEPHISTOPHELES. That was the cause, but yet by accident;
 For, when we hear one rack the name of God,
 Abjure the Scriptures and his Saviour Christ,
 We fly, in hope to get his glorious soul;
 Nor will we come, unless he use such means
 Whereby he is in danger to be damn'd.
 Therefore the shortest cut for conjuring
 Is stoutly to abjure the Trinity,
 And pray devoutly to the prince of hell.

FAUSTUS.   So Faustus hath
 Already done; and holds this principle,
 There is no chief but only Belzebub;
 To whom Faustus doth dedicate himself.
 This word 'damnation' terrifies not him,
 For he confounds hell in Elysium:
 His ghost be with the old philosophers!
 But, leaving these vain trifles of men's souls,
 Tell me what is that Lucifer thy lord?

MEPHISTOPHELES. Arch-regent and commander of all
  spirits.

FAUSTUS. Was not that Lucifer an angel once?

MEPHISTOPHELES. Yes, Faustus, and most dearly lov'd of
  God.

FAUSTUS. How comes it, then, that he is prince of devils?

MEPHISTOPHELES. O, by aspiring pride and insolence;
 For which God threw him from the face of heaven.

FAUSTUS. And what are you that live with Lucifer?

MEPHISTOPHELES. Unhappy spirits that fell with Lucifer,
 Conspir'd against our God with Lucifer,
 And are for ever damn'd with Lucifer.

FAUSTUS. Where are you damn'd?

MEPHISTOPHELES. In hell.

FAUSTUS. How comes it, then, that thou art out of hell?

MEPHISTOPHELES. Why, this is hell, nor am I out of it:
　　Think'st thou that I, who saw the face of God,
　　And tasted the eternal joys of heaven,
　　Am not tormented with ten thousand hells,
　　In being depriv'd of everlasting bliss?
　　O, Faustus, leave these frivolous demands,
　　Which strike a terror to my fainting soul!

FAUSTUS. What, is great Mephistopheles so passionate
　　For being deprivèd of the joys of heaven?
　　Learn thou of Faustus manly fortitude,
　　And scorn those joys thou never shalt possess.
　　Go bear these tidings to great Lucifer:
　　Seeing Faustus hath incurr'd eternal death
　　By desperate thoughts against Jove's deity,
　　Say he surrenders up to him his soul,
　　So he will spare him four and twenty years,
　　Letting him live in all voluptuousness;
　　Having thee ever to attend on me,
　　To give me whatsoever I shall ask,
　　To tell me whatsoever I demand,
　　To slay mine enemies, and aid my friends,
　　And always be obedient to my will.
　　Go and return to mighty Lucifer,
　　And meet me in my study at midnight,
　　And then resolve me of thy master's mind.

MEPHISTOPHELES. I will, Faustus.

　　Exit MEPHISTOPHELES.

FAUSTUS. Had I as many souls as there be stars,
　　I'd give them all for Mephistopheles.
　　By him I'll be great emperor of the world,
　　And make a bridge through the moving air,
　　To pass the ocean with a band of men;

I'll join the hills that bind the Afric shore,
And make that country continent to Spain,
And both contributory to my crown:
The Emperor shall not live but by my leave,
Nor any potentate of Germany.
Now that I have obtain'd what I desir'd,
I'll live in speculation of this art,
Till Mephistopheles return again.

Exit.

Scene Four – Preparation

The CHAPMANS' *studio. A table now stands in the middle of the room and from a metal strongbox* JAKE *is preparing each of the etchings. This is a hugely elaborate process. He wears white gloves. Each print is sealed in a plastic sleeve, which in turn is sealed in an airtight perspex box. As he removes each one he holds it up to the light and then shows it to* HELENA *who is filming.* JAKE *then passes the prints gingerly to* DINOS *who lays them on the immaculate surface of the table. He then takes three photographs of each picture. The mood is reverent and either side of the table are large unlit altar candles. Outside we can hear distant chanting. There is a sudden explosion – a window is smashed above as a brick is lobbed through a skylight.* HELENA *is startled and instinctively the* BROTHERS *smother the etchings with their bodies.*

DINOS. Somebody isn't very happy.

JAKE. Think we should go to the basement?

DINOS. They won't get in. The doors are reinforced steel.
    Anyway, the police are about.

JAKE. You sure?

DINOS. Yeah, they left a message earlier.

DINOS *presses an answerphone on the floor and, as they listen, sweeps up the glass.*

FOSTER (*on the phone*). Guys. Great piece yesterday, did you catch it on the news? Hope you were pleased – I know they edited it to look a bit hostile but that's the Beeb, eh? Pricks to a man. Anyway, do let me know when you're ready to show!

DINOS. Twat. Hold on . . .

POLICEMAN (*on the answerphone*). Hello, Mr Chapman, it's Shoreditch Police Station here . . .

DINOS. Here we go.

POLICEMAN. We've registered your concerns and received copies of both the threatening notes – very distressing for you, I'm sure, probably just kids though. Anyway, we'll send a car by to have a poke around later this evening.

JAKE. How considerate.

VOICE (*on the answerphone*). *Sint mihi dei Acherontis propitii! Valeat numen triplex Jehovoe!*

JAKE. What's that?

DINOS. Someone pissing about. Nothing.

He turns off the machine and picks up the brick. It is wrapped in paper which he reads.

Looks like this is him too. Homo Fuge.

JAKE. Eh?

DINOS. Homo Fuge. Fly, motherfucker, fly.

HELENA. Is dangerous?

JAKE. You'll be safe.

DINOS. You can always leave.

HELENA. No, I stay.

DINOS. You're brave.

HELENA. So.

DINOS. It matters.

JAKE. Have you got enough light?

HELENA. I think.

JAKE (*to* DINOS). Light the candle.

DINOS. You got a light?

JAKE. No.

DINOS. Bollocks. Matches?

JAKE. Try the drawer.

DINOS *looks*.

DINOS. Nope.

JAKE. On the sink?

DINOS. Nope.

JAKE. Check your pocket.

DINOS. I have.

JAKE. Look in mine then.

DINOS *makes a face*.

I've got the gloves on.

DINOS (*doing so*). Ooh, what is that?

JAKE. Hilarious, you are. You always have matches!

DINOS. I must have used them all.

JAKE. They were here earlier. This is ridiculous. We need to
have the candle lit to paint under the same conditions as
Goya.

DINOS. Relax. I'll nip down to the shop.

He pulls a duffle coat over his head giving him a monkish look.

I'll get a few beers to celebrate. Got any cash?

JAKE. Haven't you?

DINOS. Don't be difficult now.

JAKE. Sorry about this. You haven't got a couple of quid, have you?

HELENA. Yes. I have.

JAKE. Could we?

HELENA. Yes. Of course.

DINOS. Thanks. We'll add it to your fee.

DINOS *leaves.* JAKE *continues to work.* HELENA *films.*

JAKE. Make sure you pick up the signature.

HELENA *nods.*

Keep the focus even. Don't pan unnecessarily.

Pause.

That's better . . . So . . . you been at the BBC long?

HELENA. Is my second year.

JAKE. What else d'you cover?

HELENA. Many things. Fashion, culture, sometimes local news.

JAKE. All the dark arts then.

HELENA. Yes, we have darkroom.

JAKE. No . . . never mind. (*Beat.*) You live alone?

HELENA. Yes.

JAKE. Dinos and I used to live together but it got a bit much 24/7. You have family here?

HELENA. No.

JAKE. You're probably better off.

Pause.

HELENA. Why do you do this?

JAKE. What? The pictures?

HELENA. Yes.

JAKE. Why do you think?

HELENA. For money?

JAKE. Oh, listen, sorry about borrowing that cash. I'll write you a cheque for tonight.

HELENA. I do not want money.

JAKE. No, honestly. We'll make it up to you. It's a long night's work. Did we agree a fee?

HELENA. No, is not a problem.

JAKE. Five hundred okay?

HELENA. As you like.

JAKE. Good. (*Gesturing to pictures.*) I'll write it once I've done these.

Pause.

HELENA. This is important for you?

JAKE. The culmination of all our work. (*Looking up.*) You're an artist.

HELENA. Me? No.

JAKE. Yes you are. I can see from your composition. Your eye follows the subject – you interpret. You just don't know you're an artist yet.

HELENA. Maybe.

JAKE. Trust me – I know. I can see the way you look at these pictures. You're fascinated with them.

HELENA. I am.

JAKE. Which is your favourite?

HELENA. This. It is the worst. What does it say here?

JAKE. The title? – '*Grande hazaña! Con muertos!*' – *Great Deeds Against the Dead*. Intense, isn't it? See the way the severed limbs just hang on the tree.

Beat.

Funny you picked this one.

HELENA. Why?

JAKE. It's Dinos's favourite as well. The first time he saw it – I mean in the flesh, he actually threw up. Can you believe that?

HELENA. Yes.

JAKE. And now here they are ready for the chop. Pass me the box.

HELENA. You are happy?

JAKE. Ecstatic. That's the point. Art, making real art, makes you feel more than happy – it makes you feel alive.

HELENA. This . . . what you do . . . does not make me feel alive.

JAKE. You wait. We haven't got to the sexy bit yet.

HELENA. These pictures, I think these pictures are not 'sexy' – they are so powerful, so much hate but there is also something beautiful.

JAKE (*mocking*). Beautiful. War is not 'beautiful'.

HELENA. You know war?

JAKE. No, but I know art and that's more important.

HELENA. Art is more important than war?

JAKE. Certainly. Take these pictures. Who are these people? No one knows and no one cares. Sure, they show men and women suffering, dying but would you rather they had lived and these pictures never existed?

HELENA. This is joke?

JAKE. Not at all. I'm just trying to show you that Art is event and showbusiness. It is not some form of societal Savlon, still less social history. Shall we put the kettle on?

HELENA. Okay.

JAKE *struggles with his gloves.*

I will make.

JAKE. Tea's in the skull.

HELENA. Sorry?

JAKE. Dinos's idea. It's a *Hamlet* joke: 'Two teas or not two teas.' It's not funny . . .

HELENA. Sugar?

JAKE. That's just on the shelf. In the bag. No, that's bone meal. Yes, that one.

HELENA *makes two cups of tea.*

HELENA. I think history is important.

JAKE. Why though? Why? I mean, why is history actually important?

HELENA. Without a history we are lost. We have no meaning. We are like, how do you say, like a boat in a great ocean, lost between where we come from and where we go to.

JAKE. But this rectification will show us both places at once. Past and future.

HELENA. How can it?

JAKE. When they restore an old painting, Botticelli's *Venus*, say, the restorers take off the dust and the dirt of the past four hundred years and the world says, 'Look! Now we can see the Venus as Botticelli saw her. Isn't she beautiful!'

Bollocks! How can we see her as Botticelli saw her, through his distant, Renaissance eyes, it's impossible. We end up with a pretty picture but no knowledge of the picture's true power. Its danger. Milk's behind the brushes. What we're doing here is making something new but also recapturing something lost in the Goya – the savagery and the panic.

HELENA. You do not know this.

JAKE. No, but we'll try and then you can judge if we succeed.

HELENA. These pictures do not belong to you.

JAKE. Yes they do.

HELENA. You have them – you are lucky – but they belong to everyone.

JAKE. They were painted in the knowledge they would be sold. We now own them. We can do to them whatever we like.

HELENA. These pictures cannot fight you for their lives. They are old, weak.

JAKE. And this will make them strong again.

HELENA. These pictures are not different to you and me, they have only one life, Jake, like you.

She touches him.

I close my eyes and I see that life. Your life.

JAKE (*a little unsettled*). Then keep your eyes open. Don't look back. Do you like comics?

HELENA. Comics?

JAKE. Sit down. I've got this comic, it's an old X-Men, I think – with a story about a famous scientist, Mysterion, who had invented a machine that would read every single thought a man had. Every hope, fear, dirty dream, lost keys . . . thought. He – Mysterion – then ordered all the thoughts the man had into three categories: past, present or future. So, for example, what are you thinking of right now?

HELENA (*laughs*). Cheese sandwich. In my bag.

JAKE (*grinning*). Good, so that is a future thought, right? 'I'm imagining eating my cheese sandwich.' In the future. Understand? So now what am I thinking? I'm thinking that you must be hungry. I'm looking at your mouth and I'm thinking it's a pretty mouth but that you have bad Soviet teeth. Too much cheese. That thought of mine is a present thought, you see? So anyway, after using his machine to measure all these different thoughts that people have, Mysterion discovers that we – all humanity – divide into three types of people. Number one: those who spend most of their thoughts, most time, looking forward to the future. Number two: those who spend most thoughts in the here and now, the day to day. And number three: those who have most thoughts looking back to the past. These people outside – they are looking back. We – you and I – look forward.

HELENA. I look back now. I know people like you.

JAKE. Really?

HELENA. Yes.

In my country there is a place we call Bamiyan. This is where I come from. Is a very high place in the mountains of Afghanistan with many flowers and birds. This is a place where my people were living with much happiness. We escape war between Mujahideen and Soviet soldiers because too high for tanks. So. Then one day came Taliban to our town and everything changed. I must wear burka all day and no more study. No more camera. But worse is no music. Music is not allowed. What kind of people . . . ? They are so certain, so hard. At first they change the people but one day we hear that they must change the country too.

Bamiyan is poor, we have very little, but is famous for one thing only – the great statue of the Buddha. These statues have been in the mountain, above the town, for many hundreds of years. We say they are the guards of Bamiyan, the history but also the soul of the people. Now Taliban say they must be broken. At first they fire rockets at the statues but this is like throwing a pebble at the mountain. We say statues of Bamiyan stand against these little men and laugh. But then, all summer, Taliban lay dynamite. They are very serious now.

So it is dawn on 11th March 2001. The people are told to stay away or death, but my brother, Arun, and I decide we must see this crazy thing. Taliban may take our history but we will see them do it. We will tell the world whatever.

My brother and I climb up the valley away from the soldiers. I have camera, my brother keeps watch, and as the sun comes up we see the gold faces of the Buddhas – calm. Quiet. The Taliban like ants below. At first there is nothing, we are all alone, the sky is blue and the air clear and still. Then – Boom. Boom. The air shakes and together, two towers of dust, they fall. There were statues, beautiful statues, and now there is only a hole.

Pause.

JAKE. Yeah, I read about it. But your analogy is . . .

HELENA. This is what you do.

JAKE. No, no, it's completely different. They are asserting their ideology as a tyranny, an establishment trying to suppress any ideas contrary to theirs.

HELENA. And?

JAKE. So we: we are trying to dent the establishment, to challenge and provoke. They are fascists, we are the radicals.

HELENA. I look at these paintings and your faces of clowns and dogs, and I tell you I see dust and the kalashnikov.

JAKE. Well, maybe that's okay. Maybe my 'people' need to have their gods killed as well.

HELENA. You talk of gods and killing. What do you know of killing?

JAKE. I know what I need to, to . . .

HELENA. I tell you, if you know killing you would see these pictures and weep.

JAKE. Well, I don't . . .

HELENA (*interrupting, purposeful but matter of fact*). This day, this day when the Buddhas fall, I take many pictures. I say to my brother this will be a record for the Taliban to die one day. The dust is heavy after the explosion so I had to climb a rock to see better.

My brother . . . My brother, he is not so high. He is hungry and tired from walking. I have made him come with me and he is maybe annoyed he has missed his football game. Arun loves football. (*Beat.*) Anyway, he stops near an olive tree to eat. He has bread and some fruit. I am changing my film when I see something move near him and then there is a flash behind the tree. My brother falls very suddenly like a man praying, onto his knees. On his bread I see blood in a thick spray. He looks at me, he is only sixteen and still a boy in his face, but he shouts like an old man – 'Run' – he tries to move, he cannot and now I see – Taliban fighters with machine guns. 'Run!' There are many fighters and I run away up hill very fast, with my hands running also. Then stop. I spin round and I feel my arm is wet, from blood. I can see back by the tree is my brother.

Taliban hold him on his arms. They have a knife – he is shouting but they say nothing. They hold him tight and they just cut with knife, cut his head off. He is still alive. I know this.

JAKE. I'm sorry. This is obviously . . .

HELENA. Wait. You do not understand. Not everything. Taliban search for me but there is still smoke from the explosion so I hide in a cave in the rocks. Taliban look but cannot find me but from the cave I see. There on the tree below is my brother. Naked. They have left his body in pieces and there, on the branch, at the end, is his head.

Tell me, why do they do this?

Pause.

JAKE. I don't know.

HELENA. Why they do this – what they mean is irrelevant of
course – is nothing to you. But I will tell you – they do it
because they hate beauty. They see beauty of world, beauty
they cannot own, and so they destroy it. They are devils. I
see beauty in these pictures. I understand them. You? You see
nothing. You, little man, you are a devil.

Blackout.

Scene Five – Acts of Signature

A spotlight snaps up on FAUSTUS *with a small pile of books
and many rolls of parchment.*

FAUSTUS. Now, Faustus, must
   Thou needs be damn'd, and canst thou not be sav'd:
   What boots it, then, to think of God or heaven?
   Away with such vain fancies, and despair;
   Despair in God, and trust in Belzebub:
   Now go not backward; no, Faustus, be resolute:
   Why waver'st thou?
   O, something soundeth in mine ears,
   'Abjure this magic, turn to God again!'
   Ay, and Faustus will turn to God again.
   To God? he loves thee not;
   The god thou serv'st is thine own appetite,
   Wherein is fix'd the love of Belzebub:
   To him I'll build an altar and a church,
   And offer lukewarm blood of new-born babes.

*Above, a shadowy Barcelona gallery, 1998. We see the backs
of three sketches, each one covered with a dust sheet. Enter*
VEGA, *followed by* JAKE *and* DINOS.

VEGA. Please. Follow me, gentleman. Tell me, how was your journey?

DINOS. Fine, thanks. A little cramped.

VEGA. You travelled from Heathrow?

JAKE. No, Stansted. Ryanair.

VEGA. I did not know this airline came to Barcelona.

DINOS. It does. Dirt cheap. Not even a sandwich.

VEGA. I'm sure my assistant can arrange a bocadillo or a little tapas if you are hungry?

DINOS. Why not?

JAKE. You've just eaten!

DINOS. One paella!

VEGA (*calling*). Conchita! (*He shouts offstage in Spanish.*)

DINOS. It's cold in here.

VEGA. My apologies. We must keep our most valuable pieces at fourteen degrees centigrade for their preservation. This also accounts for the lack of natural light. I tell my wife I work in a mausoleum not an art dealers. (*Smiles.*) Anyway, Señors Chapman – to business. '*Los desastres de la guerra.*'

JAKE. *The Disasters of War.*

VEGA. *The Disasters of War.* Here, before you now, is an example of the series. They are in extraordinary condition and have not been available to public view for over twenty years. You are privileged to even see these pictures, gentleman. For reasons of security I have not brought out the whole series but I believe this selection represents a good indication of the range of Goya's style.

JAKE. Numbers thirty-six, forty-two . . .

DINOS. And thirty-nine.

VEGA. I see you are very familiar with these works.

JAKE. Oh yes.

VEGA. So.

> *Each picture has a small card in front of it with a reproduction of the sketch. He passes the first to the* BROTHERS.

Here in thirty-six we see three men hanging from a tree. The central figure is castrated. A French soldier watches, laughing, here.

> *They move to another card.*

In forty-two the subject is again a triptych – three monks stand frozen in panic as a crowd flees past them. We see remorse but also . . . guilt at their own powerlessness.

> *Another card.*

Ah. Thirty-nine. A more painterly composition, it owes something to the work of El Greco. Again the subjects are victims of French soldiers. Speculation suggests that this figure may not actually be Spanish but possibly a French traitor. As you can see the poor deserter has been decapitated.

> *Enter* GOOD ANGEL *and* EVIL ANGEL.

GOOD ANGEL. Sweet Faustus, leave that damnable art.

FAUSTUS. Contrition, prayer, repentance – what of them?

GOOD ANGEL. O, they are means to bring thee unto heaven!

EVIL ANGEL. Rather illusions, fruits of lunacy,
That make men foolish that do trust them most.

GOOD ANGEL. Sweet Faustus, think of heaven and heavenly things.

EVIL ANGEL. No, Faustus; think of honour and of wealth.

FAUSTUS. Of wealth! Why, the signiory of Embden shall be mine.
When Mephistopheles shall stand by me!

> *Exeunt* ANGELS.

VEGA. And the price . . .

A strange crackling noise disguises what he says.

. . . dollars. At auction the series would achieve perhaps five times this figure but the owner wishes to make a private sale.

Pause.

You were informed of this sum?

JAKE. We know the price.

VEGA. And it is acceptable?

DINOS. Acceptable's a bit strong . . .

VEGA. We are only here to achieve the best possible price for our client. As I say, this is less than the true market value. You are collectors or dealers?

JAKE. Artists.

VEGA. Ah. I see. And this is a substantial purchase, I suspect. What is the nature of your own art? If I may.

JAKE. We've just made a piece with a fairy in a glass jar with an erect phallus for a nose.

DINOS. It's called *Tinker Bell-End*.

VEGA. How interesting. You are not painters then?

DINOS. Painters? Look at my hands.

He holds them up – they are stained with paint.

FAUSTUS. What God can hurt thee, Faustus? Thou art safe,
  Cast no more doubts. Come, Mephistopheles,
  And bring glad tidings from great Lucifer.
  Is't not midnight? – Come, Mephistopheles,
  Veni, Veni, Mephistopheles!

JAKE. We're painting five thousand Nazi soldiers at the moment.

DINOS. To put into our new work. *Hell.*

MEPHISTOPHELES *enters. A moment.* DINOS *stares at the covered canvasses.*

VEGA. Gentleman, let me chase up your refreshments and give you a moment of privacy. Perhaps you need to discuss, hmm?

Exit VEGA.

FAUSTUS. Now tell me what says Lucifer, thy lord?

MEPHISTOPHELES. That I shall wait on Faustus whilst he lives,
So he will buy my service with his soul.

FAUSTUS. Tell me, what good will my soul do thy lord?

MEPHISTOPHELES. Enlarge his kingdom.
Tell me, Faustus, shall I have thy soul?
And I will be thy slave, and wait on thee,
And give thee more than thou hast wit to ask.

JAKE. I can't believe he's just left us with them. We could be up to anything.

DINOS. We're being watched. Look at the camera.

JAKE. Well. Shall we have a look then?

DINOS. Why not?

Gingerly, they lift the dust sheets and gaze on the sketches.

JAKE. There it is. *Great Deeds Against the Dead.*

FAUSTUS. When I behold the heavens, then I repent,
And curse thee, wicked Mephistopheles,
Because thou wouldst deprive me of those joys.

MEPHISTOPHELES. Why, Faustus,
Thinkest thou heaven is such a glorious thing?
I tell thee, 'tis not half so fair as thou,
Or any man that breathes on earth.

FAUSTUS. How prov'st thou that?

MEPHISTOPHELES. 'Twas made for man, therefore is man
    more excellent.

FAUSTUS. If it were made for man, 'twas made for me:
    I will renounce this magic and repent.

    VEGA *returns, with a tray of tapas and a book on the
    sketches.*

VEGA. Here is some light refreshment and also a history of the
    series, gentleman. It contains illustrations of all the other
    sketches. Individually they are powerful. As a series they are
    overwhelming.

FAUSTUS. My heart's so harden'd, I cannot repent:
    Scarce can I name salvation, faith, or heaven,
    But fearful echoes thunder in mine ears,
    'Faustus, thou wilt be damn'd!' then swords, and knives,
    Poison, guns, halters, and envenom'd steel
    Are laid before me to despatch myself;
    And long ere this I should have slain myself,
    Yet may not pleasure conquer deep despair.
    Will not I make blind Homer sing to me
    Of Alexander's love and Oenon's death?
    And shall not he, that built the walls of Thebes
    With ravishing sound of his melodious harp,
    Make music with my Mephistopheles?
    Why should I die, then, or basely despair?
    I am resolv'd; Faustus shall ne'er repent.
    Come, Mephistopheles, let us dispute again,
    And argue of divine astrology.

VEGA. I think you will be especially interested in the final
    fifteen plates. They are known as the '*caprichos enfáticos*'.

DINOS. 'The capricious fantasies.'

VEGA. Indeed.

FAUSTUS. Tell me, are there many heavens above the moon?

MEPHISTOPHELES. As are the elements, such are the spheres,
    Mutually folded in each other's orb,

FAUSTUS. But, tell me, have they all one motion?

MEPHISTOPHELES. All jointly move from east to west in
    twenty-four hours upon the poles of the world; but differ in
    their motion upon the poles of the zodiac.

FAUSTUS. Tush, these slender trifles any can decide:
    Hath Mephistopheles no greater skill?
    These are freshmen's suppositions.
    But, tell me, hath every sphere a dominion or intelligentia?

MEPHISTOPHELES. Ay.

FAUSTUS. How many heavens or spheres are there?

MEPHISTOPHELES. Nine.

FAUSTUS. Nine –

MEPHISTOPHELES. The seven planets.

FAUSTUS. The seven planets, the sun, the moon, Mercury,
    Venus –

MEPHISTOPHELES. Mars, Jupiter, Saturn.

FAUSTUS. The firmament.

MEPHISTOPHELES. And the empyreal heaven.

FAUSTUS. The empyreal heaven. Well I am answered.

VEGA. Aren't the titles so evocative? How is your Spanish?

DINOS (*reading*). *On Account of a Knife, What Could Be
    Worse? This is the Truth.*

FAUSTUS. And tell me, who made the world?

JAKE. So who actually owns the pictures at the moment?

MEPHISTOPHELES. I will not.

VEGA. I'm afraid I am not able to divulge this information.

FAUSTUS. Sweet Mephistopheles, tell me.

MEPHISTOPHELES. Move me not, for I will not tell thee.

FAUSTUS. Villain, have I not bound thee to tell me anything?

MEPHISTOPHELES. Think thou on hell, Faustus, for thou
shalt be damned.

FAUSTUS. Think, Faustus, upon God that made the world.

MEPHISTOPHELES. Remember this.

Exit MEPHISTOPHELES.

FAUSTUS. Ay, go, accursèd spirit, to ugly hell!
'Tis thou hast damn'd distressed Faustus' soul.

VEGA. So, gentleman, are you happy to proceed with the trans-
action?

DINOS. What d'you reckon?

JAKE. Well . . . let's do it. I think. What about you?

DINOS (*coughing slightly*). Ummm.

JAKE. You okay?

VEGA. Please, gentleman, take your time. I appreciate this is
not an easy decision and the financial implications are grave.
All I would say is life is there to be lived. Excuse me.

He exits again.

DINOS (*staring at the pictures*). *Great Deeds Against the Dead.*
Jesus.

He suddenly turns away and retches.

JAKE. Oh, that is disgusting. For Chrissake.

DINOS (*wiping his mouth*). Sorry.

JAKE. You okay?

DINOS. I don't know what's come over me.

JAKE *moves very close to* DINOS, *and takes hold of his
face.*

JAKE. Are you scared, brother?

FAUSTUS. Is't not too late?

Re-enter GOOD ANGEL *and* EVIL ANGEL.

EVIL ANGEL. Too late.

GOOD ANGEL. Never too late, if Faustus can repent.

EVIL ANGEL. If thou repent, devils shall tear thee in pieces.

GOOD ANGEL. Repent, and they shall never raze thy skin.

FAUSTUS. Arghhhhh . . .

Exeunt ANGELS. *Again,* FAUSTUS *tries to pray.* VEGA *re-enters as* DINOS *pulls himself away from* JAKE.

VEGA. I'm afraid I will need a decision, Señors Chapman. My client does not have time to waste and there are several other interested parties.

DINOS. We've decided to proceed.

VEGA. As I hoped you would! I can see you are men of an exquisite appreciation for the series. I took the liberty of anticipating your decision and have brought with me the relevant paper work. The Spanish customs and excise can be Byzantine in their complexity but we have ways and means around this.

FAUSTUS. Ah, Christ, my saviour,
Seek to save distressed Faustus' soul!

VEGA *produces a large wad of legal documentation.* JAKE *and* DINOS *take the papers and read, a little daunted. The actor playing* VEGA *becomes* LUCIFER *and enters with* MEPHISTOPHELES.

LUCIFER. Christ cannot save thy soul, for he is just:
There's none but I have interest in the same.

FAUSTUS. O, who art thou that look'st so terrible?

LUCIFER. I am Lucifer,
To whom thou wouldst bind thyself for all time.

FAUSTUS. O, Faustus, they are come to fetch away thy soul!

MEPHISTOPHELES. We come to tell thee thou dost injure us;
  Thou talk'st of Christ, contrary to thy promise:
  Thou shouldst not think of God: think of the devil.

FAUSTUS. Nor will I henceforth: pardon me in this,
  And Faustus vows never to look to heaven,
  Never to name God, or to pray to him,
  To burn his Scriptures, slay his ministers,
  And make my spirits pull his churches down.

MEPHISTOPHELES. And write a deed of gift with thine own
      blood;
  For that security craves great Lucifer.
  If thou deny it, we will back to hell.

FAUSTUS. Ay, Mephistopheles, I give it thee.

MEPHISTOPHELES. But, Faustus, thou must
  Write it in manner of a deed of gift.

FAUSTUS. Ay, so I will.

  He writes.

VEGA. The papers are all in order?

DINOS. They seem to be.

VEGA. We have no need of lawyers then. (*Smiles.*) This is the
  central contract between yourselves and the vendor. Once
  signed the purchase is complete and the money will move
  straight from your account to ours. The sale will be irre-
  versible from that moment. You are clear on this?

JAKE. Yes.

VEGA. Here is the contract.

  DINOS *reads.*

FAUSTUS. Here, Mephistopheles, receive this scroll,
  A deed of gift of body and of soul:
  But yet conditionally that thou perform
  All articles prescrib'd between us both.

MEPHISTOPHELES. Faustus, I swear by hell and Lucifer
  To effect all promises between us made!

FAUSTUS. Then hear me read them:

  'On these conditions following. First, that Faustus may be a
  spirit in form and substance. Secondly, that Mephistopheles
  shall be his servant, and at his command. Thirdly, that
  Mephistopheles shall do for him, and bring him whatsoever
  he desires. Fourthly, that he shall be in his chamber or house
  invisible. Lastly, that he shall appear to the said John
  Faustus, at all times, in what form or shape soever he please.
  I, John Faustus, of Wertenberg, Doctor, by these presents, do
  give both body and soul to Lucifer, Prince of the East, and
  his minister Mephistopheles; and furthermore grant unto
  them, that, twenty-four years being expired, full power to
  fetch or carry the said John Faustus, body and soul, flesh,
  blood, or goods, into their habitation wheresoever.'

DINOS. Seems fine.

JAKE. Good. Where do we sign?

VEGA. Allow me.

MEPHISTOPHELES. Speak, Faustus, do you deliver this as
    your deed?

FAUSTUS. Ay, take it, and the devil give thee good on't!

MEPHISTOPHELES. Then, Faustus, stab thine arm
    courageously,
  And bind thy soul, that at some certain day
  Great Lucifer may claim it as his own;
  And then be thou as great as Lucifer.

FAUSTUS (*stabbing his arm*). Lo, Mephistopheles, for love of
    thee,
  I cut mine arm, and with my proper blood
  Assure my soul to be great Lucifer's,
  Chief lord and regent of perpetual night!
  View here the blood that trickles from mine arm,
  And let it be propitious for my wish.

JAKE (*to* DINOS). Have you got a pen?

DINOS (*checking*). No.

JAKE. Typical.

DINOS. Calm down.

VEGA. I have one.

FAUSTUS. But, Mephistopheles,
　　My blood congeals, and I cannot sign.

MEPHISTOPHELES. I'll fetch thee fire to dissolve it straight.

　　JAKE *tries to write*. DINOS *tuts and has a go*.

JAKE. It's not working, I'm afraid.

VEGA. How embarrassing. I will fetch another.

　　He exits.

FAUSTUS. What might the staying of my blood portend?
　　Is it unwilling I should write this bill?
　　Why streams it not, that I may write afresh?
　　'Faustus gives to thee his soul': ah, there it stay'd!
　　Why shouldst thou not? Is not thy soul thine own?
　　Then write again, 'Faustus gives to thee his soul.'

　　Re-enter MEPHISTOPHELES *with a chafer of coals*. VEGA
　　returns with another pen.

MEPHISTOPHELES. Here's fire; come, Faustus, set it on.

FAUSTUS. So, now the blood begins to clear again.
　　Now will I make an end immediately.

VEGA. Another pen! A Swiss, so we must be happy.

　　FAUSTUS *bends down and writes in his blood. The new pen*
　　works and JAKE *signs, over and over, before allowing*
　　DINOS *to sit so he can do the same*.

FAUSTUS. *Consummatum est*; this bill is ended,
　　And Faustus hath bequeath'd his soul to Lucifer.

JAKE. That's that, then.

DINOS. Yup.

> VEGA *briskly pockets the completed contracts and presses a button on his laptop.*

VEGA. A pleasure doing business with you, gentleman. I will fetch my secretary to show you out while the handlers prepare the pictures for transit.

MEPHISTOPHELES. It is a comfort to a wretched soul to find himself a fellow in his pain.

VEGA. Please. Remember to treat them with care at all times.

DINOS. Oh, we will.

JAKE. Let's get back.

DINOS. Yes, back to hell.

> *Exit* MEPHISTOPHELES *and* VEGA *with the contracts.*
> *The* BROTHERS *approach the canvasses, remove the dust covers and stare at the sketches. As they do so, larger versions of the sketches appear and hover above the space.*
> FAUSTUS *stares at his hands.*

FAUSTUS. But what is this inscription on mine arm?
  '*Homo, fuge*': whither should I fly?
  If unto God, he'll throw me down to hell.
  My senses are deceiv'd; here's nothing writ:
  I see it plain; here in this place is writ,
  '*Homo, fuge*': yet shall not Faustus fly.

> *The light closes in on the Goyas. Blackout.*

End of Act One.

ACT TWO

Scene One – *Hell*

A pristine modern-art gallery. Three works are on display: a video installation similar to 24 Hour Psycho; The Ninth Hour *showing the Pope hit by a meteorite; and the perspex cases which make up* Hell. JAKE *and* DINOS *stand, triumphant, on a platform behind* Hell. *Around them assorted art-world-party types mill about. All is frozen and, above,* FAUSTUS *and* MEPHISTOPHELES.

MEPHISTOPHELES. Now, Faustus, ask of me what thou wilt.

FAUSTUS. First will I question with thee about hell;
    Tell me, where is the place that men call hell?

MEPHISTOPHELES. Under the heavens.

FAUSTUS. Ay, but whereabout?

MEPHISTOPHELES. Within the bowels of these elements,
    Where we are tortured and remain for ever,
    Hell hath no limits, nor is circumscribed
    In one self place; for where we are is hell,
    And where hell is, there must we ever be:
    And to conclude, when all the world dissolves,
    And every creature shall be purified,
    All places shall be hell that is not heaven.

FAUSTUS. Come, I think hell's a fable.

MEPHISTOPHELES. Ay, think so still, 'til experience change
    thy mind.

FAUSTUS. Why? Think'st thou then that Faustus shall be
    damned?

MEPHISTOPHELES. Ay, of necessity, for here's the scroll,
    Wherein thou hast given thy soul to Lucifer.

FAUSTUS. Ay, and body too, but what of that?
  Think'st thou that Faustus is so fond
  To imagine that after this life there is any pain?
  Tush; these are trifles and mere old wives' tales.

MEPHISTOPHELES. But, Faustus, I am an instance to prove
    the contrary
  For I am damned, and am now in hell.

FAUSTUS. How! Now in hell?

They disappear as the exhibition explodes into life below.

JAKE. Ladies and gentlemen. This is *Hell*. We hope you like it
  – we love it. We're very happy to be here at the Royal
  Academy. Maybe there is something important in being
  shown alongside our contemporaries. It proves we're all
  working to define our generation. The new wave breaking on
  an old shore. The aim of this installation and all our work, is
  to create art of absolutely nil cultural value. We don't believe
  art can save the depressed or enlighten the soul. Nor do we
  believe it can make the working classes more likely to appreciate IKEA. Nor do we want to make a statement about who
  we are or even why we are. That's partly why we work
  together – so you don't know whose idea is whose. The
  Chapman Brothers are depersonalised and that's the way we
  like it. We aim to make art to be consumed, analysed and dis-
  posed. That's all. Not everyone's going to like our stuff but
  they'll sure as damn recognise it as ours. That 'unsettling
  Chapman Brothers' vibe'. Have we unsettled you? Have we?
  Ask yourselves why.

DINOS (*taking the mic, he's pissed*). 'This is Hell, nor am I out
  of it.'

JAKE. Exactly. Cheers, D. Okay, that's it. Enjoy the party.

As he finishes speaking, the assembled CROWD *whoop
their approval. Circulating in their midst is* FOSTER. *He is
followed by an attractive woman,* MINTA, *who films him.
The* BROTHERS *join the party. Music.* FAUSTUS *enters,
followed by* MEPHISTOPHELES.

FAUSTUS. Nay and this be hell, I'll willingly be damned here!

MEPHISTOPHELES. Faustus, we are come to this place to
show thee some pastime: and thou shalt see all the Seven
Deadly Sins appear in their proper shapes.

FAUSTUS. That sight will be as pleasing unto me,
As Paradise was to Adam, the first day
Of his creation.

MEPHISTOPHELES. Talk not of Paradise nor creation; but
mark this show: talk of the devil, and nothing else. Come
away!

As MEPHISTOPHELES *leads* FAUSTUS *through the party,*
FOSTER *finds the* BROTHERS.

FOSTER. Jake, Dinos! How are you?

DINOS. Happy as Larry.

JAKE. Or Sally.

FOSTER. Okay! Boys, this is Minta – she's filming for me today.

DINOS. Hello, Minta.

JAKE. Who are you filming?

DINOS. Us?

FOSTER. Of course. The stars of the show. So, *Hell*. Wowey!
No one expected this from you two. It's extraordinary. All
those mini-Nazis – just amazing! Really upsetting and yet a
bit jokey too.

DINOS. That's right. We like a joke.

Pause.

Don't we, Minta?

MEPHISTOPHELES *and* FAUSTUS *approach the party
guests.*

MEPHISTOPHELES. Now, Faustus, examine them of their
several names and dispositions.

FAUSTUS (*gesturing to a guest in a suit, an art dealer*). What is he, the first?

As they are described by MEPHISTOPHELES, *each guest turns toward* FAUSTUS *and reveals themselves as a grotesque version of the sin they represent. As* MEPHISTOPHELES *finishes speaking, they snap back to reality.*

MEPHISTOPHELES. He is Covetousness and he desires that this place and all the people in it were turned to gold. O sweet gold!

FAUSTUS (*gesturing to a boy, spaced-out, druggy*). What's he, the second?

MEPHISTOPHELES. He is Sloth. He was begotten on a sunny bank, has lain there ever since and will not speak a word.

FOSTER. Once again, your work seems inspired by Goya but also it's a bit like the cover of an Iron Maiden album. More jokes?

JAKE. If we left the gags out it would look as though we cared.

FOSTER. And what's wrong with that?

JAKE. Caring implies that people can or should do something – get involved.

DINOS. That's too responsible for us. We're naughty little boys at heart.

FOSTER. As if I didn't know! So you don't want to take responsibility for the world, for your art and its effect?

JAKE. We're here to pose questions, not to provide answers.

FOSTER. Right. But doesn't the title *Hell* imply some kind of view of Good and Evil?

JAKE. No.

DINOS. We were going to call it *Fucking Hell* but the gallery wouldn't let us.

FAUSTUS (*to a drunk student*). What is he, the third?

MEPHISTOPHELES. He is Wrath. He runs up and down the world, wounding himself when he has nobody to fight withal. He was born in hell.

FOSTER. But do you both believe in hell?

JAKE. Yes, we do.

FOSTER. Sartre of course said, '*L'enfer, c'est les autres.*' 'Hell is other people.' Whatever.

He laughs too much.

What's your hell like?

JAKE (*pointedly*). It's full of people too stupid to understand our work and too ugly for us to forgive them.

DINOS (*about the installation*). But this isn't our hell. It's just a piece of art.

FOSTER. I see. It's such a complex work. So busy.

JAKE. Busy?

FOSTER. Wow, yes. Is it meant to be too huge and rambling to take in in one viewing?

JAKE (*a hint of uncertainty*). Not . . . not necessarily.

DINOS. It's meant to make you think – 'Jeez, those brothers have been working hard!'

FOSTER. No doubt about that. If there were prizes for perspiration, you boys would be quids in!

DINOS. All work and no play make Jack a dull boy!

FAUSTUS (*to a journalist*). What is she, the forth?

MEPHISTOPHELES. She's Gluttony. She comes from royal parentage. Her grandfather was a gammon of bacon, her grandmother a hogshead of claret wine. Wilt thou bidst her to supper?

FOSTER. I noticed that one of your alternative titles was *Erotic Death Throes*. Can you explain yourselves.

JAKE. It's from Freud.

FOSTER. How so? – Let's keep it simple for the folks back home.

JAKE. At its simplest, Freud claimed that there are only two forces in the world that matter: the gods Eros and Thanatos. Eros was the oldest of the gods and he was born of Chaos. Eros the maker – born out of Chaos.

FOSTER. Freaky.

JAKE. So an erotic urge is one that seeks to make or create order out of chaos.

FOSTER. *Erotic Death Throes?*

JAKE. Ah-ha. But the 'Chaos' out of which Eros emerges is the effect of Freud's other primal force, the dark god of destruction Thanatos, which seeks to destructure, to unmake, whatever has been ordered, combined and united. Look – it's all in our catalogue notes.

FOSTER (*reading*). 'The destructuring work of Thanatos functions to disunite Eros himself. Love and Strife are necessary and indestructible. Each is always present under the dominion of the other, a hint, a canker, seeping back. The opposing instincts work simultaneously: we deal never with pure life instincts or pure death instincts but only with mixtures of them in different amounts.'

JAKE. See. Erotic death throes.

FOSTER. Right!

FAUSTUS (*to* MINTA). What are you, Mistress Minx, the fifth?

MEPHISTOPHELES. Who, she, sir? She is one that follows Venus, one that will abandon reason for an inch of raw mutton. She craves only the pleasures of the body and the first letter of her name begins with 'L' . . .

FAUSTUS. A plague on her for a hot whore!

FOSTER. So finally, boys, what's caught your eye here today? Anything seem *à la mode* or new at all?

JAKE. The video installation's a bit shit but we like the Maurizio Cattelan piece.

FOSTER. Ah! The Pope struck by a meteorite? Yeah, it's great, isn't it? Religion defeated by an arbitrary universe and all that. There he is! Sorry, boys – be back later. Maurizio, it's Matthew!

FOSTER *hurries across the room, and* MEPHISTOPHELES *wheels him round to face* FAUSTUS.

FAUSTUS. What art thou, the sixth?

FOSTER. I am Envy. I cannot read and therefore wish all books were burned. I have grown lean with seeing others eat. I am Envy.

JAKE. How come I always talk more than you at these things?

DINOS. You like the sound of your own voice. 'Eros and Thanatos'!

JAKE. I'm a fucking artist, I speak in terms appropriate to art. Simplicity, blah blah . . . I'm sick of it! Did I seem nervous?

DINOS. No. You seemed arrogant.

JAKE. That's alright then. As long as I'm not becoming a parody of myself.

DINOS. You aren't becoming anything. We are becoming . . .

JAKE. What?

DINOS (*with a smile*). Famous.

FAUSTUS (*finally reaching the* BROTHERS). What art you, the seventh and last?

DINOS. I am Pride. The grandfather of vice, the violet horseman of self-love from whom all other sins arise. Cast off the grace of God and worship me. I am Pride.

FAUSTUS *and* MEPHISTOPHELES *back away and*
DINOS *returns to normal.*

JAKE. I'm so proud of this piece, you know, D. It's a love
letter.

DINOS (*grinning*). A love letter? Who to?

JAKE. To Goya of course.

DINOS. Ahhhh. The sincerest form of flattery.

JAKE. This isn't imitation, it's evolution.

MEPHISTOPHELES. Now, Faustus, how dost thou like this?

FAUSTUS. O, this feeds my soul!

MEPHISTOPHELES. Tut, Faustus, in hell is all manner of
delight.

FAUSTUS. O, might I see hell, and return again, how happy
were I then!

MEPHISTOPHELES. Thou shalt. Come away!

Exit FAUSTUS *and* MEPHISTOPHELES.

DINOS. Do you believe in hell?

Beat.

JAKE. I think I do.

DINOS. And what's it really like?

JAKE. Hell? Hell is having nothing to say.

DINOS. Not pits of desperate sinners flailing in burning oil,
then?

JAKE (*ignoring him*). Or maybe worse – having something to
say but not being able to say it clearly.

DINOS. Yes. That would be the pits.

Beat. He notices JAKE *fidgeting.*

What's the matter now?

JAKE. I dunno. These openings. No one ever actually pays any attention.

DINOS. They will.

JAKE. I hope so.

DINOS. Trust me.

JAKE. D, about Barcelona.

DINOS. Forget it.

JAKE. It was just the heat, you know, the tension.

DINOS. Seriously. Forget it. I have.

Pause.

What d'you wanna do now?

JAKE. Let's get pissed!

DINOS. Now you're talking! I do like this Pope, though.

JAKE. He's hilarious.

A moment as JAKE *and* DINOS *stand over the slain* POPE *and chuckle to themselves, it's a good joke. They leave.*

Scene Two – The Pope and the Prize

Slowly, the POPE *lifts the rock, stands up and dusts himself down. Lights rise on a table, laden with food and wine. Organ music and, in the distance, chanting. The* POPE *takes his place in the centre of the table and freezes. The Hitchcock video installation suddenly clicks into real time and the actress addresses the audience.*

VIDEO CHORUS. Learnèd Faustus,
To learn the secrets of astronomy,
Did mount him up to scale Olympus' top;

Where sitting in a chariot burning bright,
Drawn by the strength of yokèd dragons' necks,
He views the clouds, the planets, and the stars,
The tropics, zones and quarters of the sky . . .

The screen goes static, then off. Enter FAUSTUS *and*
MEPHISTOPHELES.

FAUSTUS. Having now, my good Mephistopheles,
Pass'd with delight the stately town of Trier,
Environ'd round with airy mountain-tops,
With walls of flint, and deep-entrenched lakes,
From Paris next, coasting the realm of France,
We saw the river Maine fall into Rhine,
Whose banks are set with groves of fruitful vines;
Then up to Naples, rich Campania,
Whose buildings fair and gorgeous to the eye,
The streets straight forth, and pav'd with finest brick,
Quarter the town in four equivalents:
There saw we learnèd Maro's golden tomb,
The way he cut, an English mile in length,
Through a rock of stone, in one night's space;
From thence to Venice, Padua, and the rest,
In one of which a sumptuous temple stands,
That threats the stars with her aspiring top.
Thus hitherto hath Faustus spent his time:
But tell me now what resting place is this?
Hast thou, as erst I did command,
Conducted me within the walls of Rome?

MEPHISTOPHELES. Faustus, I have; and, because we will not
be unprovided, I have taken up his Holiness' privy chamber
for our use.

FAUSTUS. I hope his Holiness will bid us welcome.

MEPHISTOPHELES. Tut, 'tis no matter, man; we'll be bold
with his good cheer.

FAUSTUS. Well, I'm content to compass then some sport,
And by his folly make us merriment.

Then charm me, that I
May be invisible, to do what I please,
Unseen of any whilst I stay in Rome.

MEPHISTOPHELES *charms him.*

MEPHISTOPHELES. So, Faustus; now
Do what thou wilt, thou shalt not be discern'd.

MEPHISTOPHELES *claps his hands and a party of*
FRIARS *enter, slowly chanting. They reach the table and sit*
with the POPE, *who bursts into life.* FAUSTUS *watches.*

POPE. My Lords of Lorrain, will't please you draw near?

FAUSTUS (*whispering*). Fall to, and the devil choke you, an
you spare!

POPE. How now! Who's that which spake? Friars, look about.

FIRST FRIAR. Here's nobody, if it like your Holiness.

POPE. My lord, (*Coughs.*) here is a dainty dish was sent me
from the Bishop of Milan.

FAUSTUS. I thank you, sir.

POPE. How now! Who's that which snatched the meat from
me? Will no man look? My lord, I'll drink to your grace.

FAUSTUS. I'll pledge your grace.

He pours wine over the POPE.

POPE. My lord, this dish was sent me from the Cardinal of Flo-
rence.

FAUSTUS. You say true; I'll ha't.

He pushes a cream pie into the POPE*'s face.*

SECOND FRIAR. My lord, it may be some ghost, newly crept
out of Purgatory, come to beg a pardon of your Holiness.

POPE. It may be so. Friars, prepare a dirge to lay the fury of
this ghost. Once again, my lord, fall to.

The POPE *crosses himself.*

FAUSTUS. What, are you crossing of yourself? Well, use that trick no more, I would advise you.

The POPE *crosses himself again.*

Well, there's the second time. Aware the third; I give you fair warning.

The POPE *crosses himself again, and* FAUSTUS *boxes him on the ear. The* FRIARS *scatter. The* POPE *climbs on top of the table.*

Come on, Mephistopheles; what shall we do?

The FRIARS *form themselves into a mass around the table and begin chanting. They rise and fall as a group three times and when they rise again the* POPE *is replaced by* FOSTER. *The* FRIARS *throw off their cloaks and become the art-world characters from the previous scene.*

FOSTER (*shouting to make himself heard*). Ladies, gentlemen, and Madonna! Well, here we are again and a very warm welcome to Tate Britain and the Turner Prize 2001. Golly gosh! Each year the Turner tends to cause a stir and – surprise, surprise – today is no exception. So, in 2001 what's going down? Well, we have a Margate maiden's unmade bed, a lighting installation by the king of Minimalism, a set of lo-fi family photos, and two brothers who have made a model of five thousand mutilated Nazis. As my American friends would say, 'Go figure.'

People often ask me, 'What would Turner have had to say about the Turner Prize?', and I always reply that he would have undoubtedly appreciated the new ways of looking at things that the late twentieth century has granted artists. I actually say Turner would have loved the Turner Prize. It's about acknowledging that art is worth celebrating and worth perfecting – and so the nominations this year are: Tracey Emin for *My Bed*. Martin Creed for *The Lights Going On and Off*. Richard Billingham for *Ray's A Laugh*. And the Chapman Brothers for *Hell*.

And the winner is . . . Martin Creed for *The Lights Going On and Off!*

The CROWD *erupts with cheering, applause.*

DINOS. Bollocks.

JAKE. Hmmm.

DINOS. Bollocks. Bollocks. Bollocks.

FOSTER. *The Lights Going On and Off* is what is known in the art world as a Ronseal work, i.e. it does exactly what it says on the tin. Some people say that the piece is only an idea and never needed to be made. A joke almost. What does it mean? These flashing lights? These strange pulses of light? Who knows? Perhaps it makes us think of space and rooms differently? Perhaps it's about the random flicker of life? Perhaps it's just some lights on a wall? Anyway, while Martin can't be here to talk about his work, it is of course installed in this room and without further ado, let's see it in action. Hit it!

The wall lights begin a cycle, first bright white, then so all are in silhouette, then off. This repeats. The CROWD *and* FOSTER *surge offstage. Remaining are* JAKE *and* DINOS, *slightly deflated, sitting to one side and to the other, an* OLD MAN, *either passed-out drunk or asleep.*

JAKE. Well, that's that then.

DINOS. Seems to be.

JAKE. Another year gone.

DINOS. Yes.

JAKE. The Turner! Crap wine and Charles Saatchi.

DINOS. Did you talk to him?

JAKE. Yeah. He thought it was ours.

DINOS. Oh good.

JAKE. In fact, Matt says he's ready to make an offer for *Hell.*

DINOS. Excellent! Christ knows we need the cash after the . . .

JAKE. The Goyas. Yes, I know.

DINOS (*sighs*). The Goyas. Ah well, the prize money would have been handy.

Pause.

I enjoyed the vol-au-vents though.

JAKE. You had vol-au-vents?

DINOS. Didn't you?

JAKE. Nah, sausage rolls.

DINOS. Oh well. The vol-au-vents were the best.

JAKE. They were good?

DINOS. Fabulous.

JAKE. Really?

DINOS. Why would I lie to you?

JAKE. I suppose.

DINOS. Yes, the vol-au-vents were excellent.

JAKE. So I gather.

DINOS. The vol-au-vents were the winners by far.

JAKE. Unlike us.

DINOS. Yes.

He kicks the OLD MAN.

OLD MAN (*mumbled*). When Ruskin was a boy . . .

Pause.

JAKE. It would be easier if it were an injustice. What makes it so infuriating is that we were beaten by such a good piece.

DINOS. It's very good. Very moving.

JAKE. Why is that?

DINOS. Not sure. Its simplicity. Makes me feel calm and dangerous at the same time.

JAKE. It reminds me of when you used to stop me reading in bed.

DINOS. When we were kids.

JAKE. You and that light switch!

DINOS. The privilege of the younger.

JAKE. Hmmm.

DINOS. So. What do we learn?

JAKE. Learn?

DINOS. From this.

JAKE. Well. 'Keep it simple –

DINOS. – stupid.'

JAKE. Here we are busting our guts with five thousand hand-painted miniatures and along comes Martin with his little lights.

DINOS. Yes.

JAKE. It's so pure. Doesn't need any bloody catalogue notes – Creed doesn't even have to turn up and explain himself. It's just here.

DINOS. Yes.

JAKE. So absolutely the essence of what he does. It's like a haiku.

For a moment they consider this. FAUSTUS *wanders back on stage. His coat is tattered, dirtied, bloody. He looks older.*

FAUSTUS. Faustus, thou hast with pleasure ta'en the view
Of rarest things, and royal courts of kings,
Thou stay'd thy course, and so return thee home;
Where such as bear my absence but with grief,
I mean my friends and near'st companions,

Did gratulate my safety with kind words,
And in their conference of what befell,
Touching my journey through the world and air,
They put forth questions of astrology,
Which Faustus answer'd with such learnèd skill
As they admir'd and wonder'd at my wit.
Now is my fame spread forth in every land
And yet, old Faustus, fear the restless course
That time doth run with calm and silent foot,
Shortening thy days and thread of vital life,
Calling for payment of thy latest years.

JAKE. That's the problem with us. With *Hell*.

DINOS. With *Hell*? What the hell d'you mean?

JAKE. It's all there.

DINOS. And proudly so.

JAKE. Yes, but it's too much. Too bloated.

DINOS. Good. And . . .

JAKE. It's not ambiguous. There's nothing unknown about it.
No mystery. No cryptic simplicity.

DINOS. Nothing simple about all that modelling.

JAKE. Exactly. The workmanship was worthy, not challenging.
Like the Sistine Chapel.

DINOS. I quite like the Sistine Chapel.

JAKE. Yes, but it doesn't ask anything of the viewer. There it is
on the ceiling. 'Isn't it impressive?' you say. 'Isn't it beautiful!' But the effort is exhausting, self-conscious. A good
work of art . . .

DINOS. Like this work of art.

JAKE. . . . uses its economy to remove the artist from the equa-
tion. The question is put directly to the viewer and it is a
question that asks us who we are, what we are.

FAUSTUS. What art thou, Faustus, but a man condemn'd to
     die?
   Thy fatal time doth draw to final end;
   Despair doth drive distrust into my thoughts:
   Confound these passions with a quiet sleep:
   Tush, Christ did call the thief upon the cross;
   Then rest thee, Faustus, quiet in conceit.

   FAUSTUS *collapses into a chair next to the drunk and
   sleeping* OLD MAN.

DINOS. Look, someone's scribbled on the wall.

JAKE. What does it say?

DINOS. 'What a load of crap.'

JAKE. A critic and a poet.

DINOS. This kind of work always gets in people's faces. It's an
   idea. People hate ideas. Especially new ones.

JAKE. Exactly. The *Daily Mail* will kill this piece tomorrow,
   The Lights Going On and Off. That's all it is. It's brilliant!
   The *Daily Mail* will murder it!

DINOS. Is that why we love it?

JAKE. That's why it's better than us.

   The OLD MAN *rises suddenly.*

OLD MAN. O, gentle Faustus, leave this damnèd art,
   This magic, that will charm thy soul to hell,
   And quite bereave thee of salvation.
   Though thou hast now offended like a man,
   Do not persever in it like a devil.
   Yet, yet thou hast an amiable soul,
   If sin by custom enters not your nature;
   Then, Faustus, will repentance come too late,
   Then thou art banished from the sight of heaven;
   No mortal can express the pains of hell.
   It may be this my exhortation
   Seems harsh, and all unpleasant; let it not,

For, gentle friend, I speak it not in wrath,
Or envy of thee, but in tender love,
And pity of thy future misery.
And so have hope, that this my kind rebuke,
Checking thy body, may amend thy soul.

DINOS. What now?

JAKE. Keep going.

DINOS. There's always more.

JAKE. Until there's nothing.

DINOS. Be better.

JAKE. And never be good enough?

DINOS. God forbid!

JAKE. I don't know if I've got it in me. I just don't know if it's there.

DINOS. Come home. Let's sleep on it. There's always time.

FAUSTUS. Where art thou, Faustus? Wretch, what hast thou done?
Damn'd art thou, Faustus, damn'd; despair and die!
Hell calls for right, and with a roaring voice
Says, 'Faustus, come; thine hour is almost come.'
And Faustus now will come to do thee right.

OLD MAN. Ah, stay, good Faustus, stay thy desperate steps!
I see an angel hovers o'er thy head,
And, with a vial full of precious grace,
Offers to pour the same into thy soul:
Then call for mercy, and avoid despair.

FAUSTUS. Ah, my sweet friend, I feel
Thy words to comfort my distressed soul!
Leave me a while to ponder on my sins.

OLD MAN. I go, sweet Faustus; but with heavy cheer,
Fearing the ruin of thy hopeless soul.

Exit OLD MAN.

JAKE. Cup of tea when we get in?

DINOS. Oh yes. And a Jaffa Cake.

JAKE. No. You know what?

DINOS. What?

JAKE. Let's have a proper drink and get the Goyas out.

DINOS. The Goyas?

JAKE. Yeah. I think we could find a little inspiration there.

DINOS. Always.

JAKE. Yes. Tonight I feel like I'm ready to look at them properly.

The BROTHERS *leave.* FAUSTUS *stands.*

FAUSTUS. The serpent that tempted Eve may be saved, but not Faustus. O, gentlemen, hear with patience, and tremble not at my speeches. Though my heart pant and quiver to remember that I have been a student here these thirty years, O would I had never seen Wertenberg, never read book. And what wonders I have done, all Germany can witness, yea, all the world, for which Faustus hath lost both Germany and the world, yea heaven itself, heaven, the seat of God, the Throne of the Blessed, the Kingdom of Joy, and must remain in hell for ever. Hell, O, hell for ever.

Gentlemen, farewell. If I live 'til morning, I'll visit you; if not, Faustus is gone to hell.

As he leaves, the light sequence turns off, plunging the stage into darkness.

Scene Three – Now Must Thou Needs Be Damned

The CHAPMANS' *studio at the moment we left it in Act One. We can again hear the distant protest outside.*

HELENA. You, little man, you are a devil.

Long pause.

JAKE (*evenly*). Look, Helena, I'm sorry about your brother. Truly. But this is emotional blackmail, not an argument . . .

HELENA. No!

JAKE. Yes, it is! I can understand that our . . . that this thing we're doing means something more to . . . after your brother's death. But this is only art.

HELENA. Nothing is only art. You think you understand these. You understand nothing. Do you know the sound a man makes when they cut through his neck? It is a sigh, a sigh of blood from the windpipe as it opens. I have heard that sigh. These pictures have heard that sigh. You? You can only imagine it.

JAKE. But everything dies eventually! The life of a work of art is as fixed as a man's.

HELENA. You only say this because you know I am right. I see in your eyes. You are frightened of not being good enough. Of being gone and no one remembering you, of your immortality – over this you have no power. But you cannot create and so you destroy.

Pause.

JAKE. Keep your opinions to yourself. You're here to do a job. If you don't like it, leave.

HELENA. It is not me who does not like this, Jake. It is you too.

JAKE. It's too late.

JAKE moves away from her, back to his pictures. DINOS *returns with matches and beer.*

DINOS. How's it going?

JAKE (*pulling himself together a little*). Fine. Nearly ready.

DINOS (*lighting the candles*). It's hilarious out there. There's actually a little protest going down on the street corner. This thing is going to be huge! This was a good idea of yours.

JAKE. Was it my idea?

DINOS. Hell, yeah! The night after the Turner, remember?

JAKE. I'd forgotten.

DINOS. What you been up to?

JAKE. Just talking.

DINOS. Mix the paint.

JAKE. Right.

DINOS (*holding up a CD*). I also got this out of the car! A little light listening for us to work to!

JAKE. Put it on.

DINOS. Sorry?

JAKE. I said put it on.

DINOS (*reading the sleeve notes*). You know AKA are DJing tonight?

JAKE. DJing?

DINOS. The party . . . remember.

JAKE. Oh right. Right.

DINOS. Siberian trance no doubt . . .

JAKE. Yeah.

DINOS. . . . or Montenegran hardstep!

JAKE. . . . Um . . . d'you want another look at the . . . the series. I've er . . . I've prepped the paint.

DINOS. You alright?

JAKE. Fine. I just . . . well, d'you want a look?

DINOS. In case I change my mind?

JAKE. Well?

DINOS (*grinning*). I don't think so.

A moment to take in the series.

Don't they look fantastic! Like Joan of Arc at the stake.

JAKE. We're not burning them.

DINOS. Of course not. It's awful not to be loved . . . makes you mean and violent and cruel.

JAKE. What?

DINOS. It was the last thing James Dean said before he died. Well, actually the last thing he said was probably, 'Fucking Treeeeeee!' but it was the last thing he said on film. You know that, Helena?

HELENA. No.

DINOS. 'It's awful not to be loved . . . makes you mean and violent and cruel.' Let me tell you – this series is James Dean. You know why? Because they leave the world beautiful and age – age shall not weary them.

He dances.

Hey, Helena, dance with me.

He gathers her up.

See, I'm irresistible.

They nearly bump into the table.

JAKE. Careful!

DINOS. Helena, will you be the mother of our children?

HELENA. Please . . .

DINOS. All children need mothering.

HELENA. Stop . . .

DINOS. These babies we're making tonight will cry out for you. Mummy.

JAKE. Leave her alone.

DINOS (*doing so*). Quite right, let's concentrate. After all, the midwife can't be drunk on the job. Have you got the puppy and clown sketches?

JAKE (*gesturing*). They're here.

DINOS. God. (*Beat.*) I'd forgotten how upsetting they are.

JAKE. Too much?

DINOS. No . . . no way!

JAKE. You sure?

DINOS. What are you talking about?

JAKE. Are they too much?

DINOS. How can they be too upsetting? It's like asking if this knife is too sharp. (*Playing with the blade.*) It's a knife – it's meant to be sharp. (*Pricks himself.*) Oww!

He puts it down.

JAKE. You don't think the faces will be a bit . . .

DINOS. What?

JAKE. Er . . . demeaning.

DINOS. Demeaning?

JAKE. Yes.

DINOS. What? What are you talking about? (*Beat.*) I don't believe this! You're bottling, aren't you? What's going on?

JAKE. I'm not. I'm not!

DINOS. Really?

JAKE. Y . . . yes.

DINOS. Show me your hands. You're shaking!

FAUSTUS *is revealed above.*

FAUSTUS. Accursèd Faustus, where is mercy now?
  I do repent; and yet I do despair:
  Hell strives with grace for conquest in my breast:
  What shall I do to shun the snares of death?

Suddenly, MEPHISTOPHELES *is next to him.* FAUSTUS
screams.

MEPHISTOPHELES. O, thou hast lost celestial happiness,
  Pleasures unspeakable, bliss without end.
  Hadst thou affected sweet divinity,
  Hell or the devil had had no power on thee.
  Hadst thou kept on that way Faustus, behold,
  In what resplendent glory thou hadst set
  In yonder throne, like those bright shining saints,
  And triumphed over hell. That hast thou lost.
  The jaws of hell are open to receive thee.
  Now, Faustus, let thine eyes with horror stare
  Into that vast perpetual torture-house.
  There are the Furies tossing damned souls,
  On burning forks; their bodies broil in lead.
  There are live quarters broiling on the coals,
  That ne'er can die. This ever-burning chair,
  Is for o'er-tortured souls to rest them in.
  But yet all these are nothing; thou shalt see
  Ten thousand tortures that more horrid be.

DINOS. What's she been saying?

JAKE. Nothing.

DINOS. Helena? What have you been s . . .

JAKE. It's not her. I just wonder if we shouldn't wait a bit
  longer.

DINOS. Wait . . .

JAKE. Yes.

DINOS. Why?

JAKE. I . . . I've been thinking.

HELENA. We have been talking.

DINOS. Oh really?

JAKE. D, look at these pictures. They're made by someone who's seen things we can only imagine. Real suffering. I don't know if we –

DINOS. What?

JAKE. . . . are entitled to do this.

DINOS. Entitled? I can't believe this. Entitled!

JAKE. Yes.

DINOS. What entitles us is our rights as artists, as owners and as revolutionaries! Jaaaake! This is the Chapman Brothers! Not the Neville Brothers, not the Chuckle Brothers but the Chapman Brothers! Very funny! You're having a laugh, right? For a moment I almost . . . (*Beat.*) Jake?

JAKE. D. We, you and I, we had an idea, a great idea . . .

DINOS. A major idea!

JAKE. I know . . .

DINOS. An idea, let me remind you that started with you!

JAKE. I know, but can we say we've felt these things? That we understand real suffering?

DINOS. I'm more than happy to help you understand a little suffering! This is a sentimental argument! It's a wet argument!

JAKE. We have a duty to . . .

DINOS. A duty! Sure we have a duty – our duty to each other. Our duty to twenty years of work.

JAKE. This is different. It's permanent. If there's doubt then we must stop.

FAUSTUS. O my God, I would weep, but the devil draws in my tears! Gush forth blood instead of tears, yea, life and soul. Oh, he stays my tongue. I would lift up my hands, but see, they hold 'em, they hold 'em!

MEPHISTOPHELES. Thou traitor, Faustus, I arrest thy soul
For disobedience to my sovereign lord:
Revolt, or I'll in piece-meal tear thy flesh.

JAKE. Anyway, you're in no state to paint . . .

DINOS. I'm in no state . . .

JAKE. We need to be calm . . .

DINOS. Calm! Calm! You're about to fuck our whole reputation and you want calm . . .

JAKE. Look . . .

DINOS. What's got into you?

JAKE. I . . .

DINOS. Jake, have you always been scared?

JAKE. No . . .

DINOS. A small part of you . . .

JAKE. No . . .

DINOS. The money . . .

JAKE. No.

DINOS. Then what's going on here!

JAKE. I just feel . . .

DINOS. You feel!

JAKE. I think that we are in danger of . . .

DINOS. This better be good . . .

JAKE. . . . in danger of losing sight of what . . .

DINOS. Come on!

JAKE. . . . of what is beautiful in these works . . .

DINOS. Of what is! Of what is beautiful . . .

JAKE. Yes.

DINOS. Jake, what's happened to you?

JAKE. I know it's not what we agreed – and I'm not even sure
    myself – but shouldn't we hold fire until we are.

DINOS. I AM SURE!

HELENA. He has changed his mind. Is that so hard for you?

DINOS. Who . . . who is she, Jake?

HELENA. I am not . . .

DINOS. What's she done to you? She give you something?

JAKE. Don't be ridiculous.

DINOS. In the tea? Ketamine? Rohypnol? Let me see your
    eyes.

JAKE. Get off!

DINOS. You can just never keep your cock in your pants, can
    you?

JAKE. What?

DINOS. It's pathetic. I mean, at your age!

JAKE. Fuck off!

DINOS. Is that what this is? Love? Have you fallen in love, big
    brother?

HELENA. Please . . .

DINOS. I think you've done quite enough.

He pushes HELENA *offstage into the kitchen and turns to* JAKE.

Jake, now, Jake, I'm going to take the liberty of reminding you of a few little things you seem to have decided to forget.

JAKE. Let her out . . .

DINOS. Shut-the-fuck-up. For once, I'll do the talking.

FAUSTUS. Sweet Mephistopheles, entreat thy lord
    To pardon my unjust presumption,
    And with my blood again I will confirm
    My former vow I made to Lucifer.

MEPHISTOPHELES. Do it, then, quickly, with unfeignèd
        heart,
    Lest greater danger do attend thy drift.

FAUSTUS. Torment, sweet friend, that base and crooked age,
    That durst dissuade me from thy Lucifer,
    With greatest torments that our hell affords.

MEPHISTOPHELES. His faith is great; I cannot touch his soul;
    But what I may afflict his body with
    I will attempt, which is but little worth.

DINOS. Jake, listen to me, I'll speak as slowly as I can.

JAKE. Okay.

DINOS. We haven't come this far to pull out now. If we do, understand this, we are yesterday's news, we are the nearly men, the Tim Hen-men of the art world, we are never – repeat never – going to sell a piece of art again. Okay. This girl has come here, she's a beautiful girl, we both know that, we could both see that. Fine. She comes here and wants to change your mind. That's her agenda. She wants to come between us.

JAKE. Why?

DINOS. Like the fuck I know. I don't know. A bit of attention. Maybe she's a secret Spaniard. Maybe she's a friend of Brian

Sewell's, maybe she's just envious of all the attention we're getting. The point is, she's made you lose sight of the prize. Yes?

JAKE. I . . . I . . .

DINOS. Jakey, look into my eyes. Look. We are on the verge of making history; if we don't do this, we are history. Step up to the mark and be counted.

FAUSTUS. One thing, good servant, let me crave of thee,
    To glut the longing of my heart's desire,
    That I might have unto my paramour
    That heavenly Helen which I saw of late,
    Whose sweet embracings may extinguish clean
    Those thoughts that do dissuade me from my vow,
    And keep mine oath I made to Lucifer.

MEPHISTOPHELES. Faustus, this, or what else thou shalt desire,
    Shall be perform'd in twinkling of an eye.

DINOS. So we carry on. Yes?

JAKE. Okay.

DINOS. You understand it has to be tonight.

JAKE. Uh-huh.

DINOS. Tonight has been set and fixed for weeks. If not tonight then never.

JAKE. I know.

DINOS. Jakey. It's me. I know you like this girl but she's just a pretty bit of exotica. No more. Don't get carried away. It's the nerves.

JAKE. I know. I'm all blurry. It's just . . . I feel . . .

DINOS. What. What?

JAKE. Guilt?

DINOS. Guilt! What is this? Confession?

JAKE. I feel sordid.

DINOS. And so you should. How d'you think Goya felt when he sat down to make these? Eh? This – this is where courage begins.

JAKE. Courage.

DINOS. Yes. Courage. Suffering doesn't validate the work, Jake. It doesn't make it any more real. If it did, then rape and torture would be the first module at art school. It's imagination that validates the work, Jake. Goya didn't hurt any more than Mr and Mrs Sanchez next door. He just imagined more. Okay? You sure?

JAKE *nods*.

That's my boy.

Beat.

Okay, Yoko, you can come back in now – we need you on the camera.

He lets HELENA *back in*.

Be a good girl now.

DINOS *goes to the table and sits*. FAUSTUS *stares ahead of himself, into the void, transfixed. Below,* JAKE *slowly approaches* HELENA *who doesn't react.*

FAUSTUS. Was this the face that launch'd a thousand ships,
And burnt the topless towers of Ilium?
Sweet Helen, make me immortal with a kiss.

JAKE. Her lips suck forth my soul: see where it flies!
Come, Helen, come, give me my soul again.
Here will I dwell.

FAUSTUS.   For heaven is in these lips,
And all is dross that is not Helena.

JAKE. I will be Paris, and for love of thee,
Instead of Troy,

FAUSTUS.   Shall Wertenberg be sack'd;

JAKE. Yea, I will wound Achilles in the heel,
    And then return to Helen for a kiss.
    O, thou art fairer than the evening air
    Clad in the beauty of a thousand stars;

FAUSTUS. And none but thou shalt be my paramour!
    Fair is too foul an epithet for thee,
    With hair dishevell'd wiping thy watery cheeks;
    There Beauty, mother to the Muses, sits,
    Taking instructions from thy flowing eyes;
    There angels in their crystal armours fight
    A doubtful battle with my tempted thoughts.

JAKE *and* FAUSTUS (*together*). What is beauty –

FAUSTUS.   – saith my sufferings, then?
    If all the pens that ever poets held
    Had fed the feeling of their masters' thoughts,
    And all combin'd in beauty's worthiness,

JAKE. Yet should there hover in their restless heads.

FAUSTUS. One thought,

JAKE.   one grace,

FAUSTUS.   one wonder, at the least,

JAKE. Which into words no virtue can digest,
    With whose instinct the soul of man is touch'd;

FAUSTUS. And every warrior that is rapt with love
    Of fame,

JAKE.   of valour,

FAUSTUS.   and of victory,

JAKE. Must needs have

BOTH.   beauty

FAUSTUS.   beat on his conceits.

A long moment as JAKE *almost reaches out to touch*
HELENA. *He suddenly snaps out of it, shaking his head.*
Lights snap off on FAUSTUS.

JAKE. Get out.

HELENA. What?

JAKE. Get out. Just leave.

HELENA. Jake, I don't understand . . .

DINOS. You heard him.

HELENA. Look at me, Jake.

DINOS. You're not listening, angel.

JAKE. We'll film ourselves.

HELENA. Look at me!

DINOS. Hey, maybe he's too busy right now!

JAKE (*looking at* HELENA). Go. I want you to go.

Pause.

HELENA. Yes, I go. I will not be a part of this any more.

DINOS. But leave your camera behind.

JAKE. I just can't do this with you here. I'm sorry.

HELENA *looks at the series and slowly makes to leave. Sud-*
denly she hurls herself at the table, picks up the knife and
impales JAKE's *hand. He roars in pain but* DINOS *leaps in*
her way and there is a tussle. JAKE *covers the sketches as*
DINOS *picks* HELENA *up and drags her out. We hear the*
CROWD *yell as the door is opened. A long pause.* JAKE
pulls the knife from his hand and watches the blood drip
down his arm. DINOS *returns, out of breath. They look at*
one another. JAKE *slowly passes* DINOS *a brush and*
together they turn to the table.

Put the camera on me.

DINOS *does so.*

We're going to do this now. Will it be any good? That's up to
you. You have been watching the Chapman Brothers.

DINOS. Goodnight.

Darkness. Then FAUSTUS, *in the chair, above.*

FAUSTUS. Ah, Faustus,
   Now hast thou but one bare hour to live,
   And then thou must be damn'd perpetually!
   Stand still, you ever-moving spheres of heaven,
   That time may cease, and midnight never come;
   Fair Nature's eye, rise, rise again, and make
   Perpetual day; or let this hour be but
   A year, a month, a week, a natural day,
   That Faustus may repent and save his soul!
   O lente, lente currite noctis equi!
   The stars move still, time runs, the clock will strike,
   The devil will come, and Faustus must be damn'd.
   O, I'll leap up to my God! – Who pulls me down? –
   See, see, where Christ's blood streams in the firmament!
   One drop would save my soul, half a drop: ah, my Christ! –
   Ah, rend not my heart for naming of my Christ!
   Yet will I call on him: O, spare me, Lucifer! –
   Where is it now? 'Tis gone: and see, where God
   Stretcheth out his arm, and bends his ireful brows!
   Mountains and hills, come, come, and fall on me,
   And hide me from the heavy wrath of God!
   No, no!
   Then will I headlong run into the earth:
   Earth, gape! O, no, it will not harbour me!
   You stars that reign'd at my nativity,
   Whose influence hath allotted death and hell,
   Now draw up Faustus, like a foggy mist.
   Into the entrails of yon labouring cloud,
   That, when you vomit forth into the air,
   My limbs may issue from your smoky mouths,
   So that my soul may but ascend to heaven!

Bells chime.

Ah, half the hour is past! 'Twill all be past anon
O God,
If thou wilt not have mercy on my soul,
Yet for Christ's sake, whose blood hath ransom'd me,
Impose some end to my incessant pain;
Let Faustus live in hell a thousand years,
A hundred thousand, and at last be sav'd!
O, no end is limited to damnèd souls!
Why wert thou not a creature wanting soul?
Or why is this immortal that thou hast?
Ah, Pythagoras' *metempsychosis*, were that true,
This soul should fly from me, and I be chang'd
Unto some brutish beast!
All beasts are happy, for, when they die,
Their souls are soon dissolv'd in elements;
But mine must live still to be plagu'd in hell.
Cursed be the parents that engender'd me!
No, Faustus, curse thyself, curse Lucifer
That hath depriv'd thee of the joys of heaven.

The clock strikes midnight.

O, it strikes, it strikes! Now, body, turn to air,
Or Lucifer will bear thee quick to hell!
O soul, be chang'd into little water-drops,
And fall into the ocean, ne'er be found!

Behind FAUSTUS, MEPHISTOPHELES *is revealed in
flames. He approaches the back of the chair.*

My God, my God, look not so fierce on me!
Adders and serpents, let me breathe a while!
Ugly hell, gape not! Come not, Lucifer!
I'll burn my books! – Ah, Mephistopheles!

We see an overhead shot of JAKE *and* DINOS *as they apply
the very first touches of paint. As they do so,*
MEPHISTOPHELES *reaches* FAUSTUS *and clamps a
clown mask over his screaming face. On either side of him,*

the Goya sketches appear in the air, now in their rectified state. Lights fade on JAKE *and* DINOS *silently painting, then on* FAUSTUS *and finally on the Goyas. A projection:*

'*In 2004 a mysterious fire broke out in a London warehouse and many important pieces of modern British art were destroyed. Amongst the items lost in the flames was the Chapman Brothers' 1999 installation* Hell. *Their rectified Goya sketches,* Insult to Injury, *survive.*'

The End.

A Nick Hern Book

Faustus first published in Great Britain as a paperback original in 2007 by Nick Hern Books Limited, 14 Larden Road, London W3 7ST, in association with Headlong Theatre

Faustus copyright © 2007 Rupert Goold and Ben Power

Rupert Goold and Ben Power have asserted their right to be identified as the authors of this work

Cover image: Eureka!, www.eureka.co.uk

Typeset by Nick Hern Books, London
Printed in the UK by CPI Bookmarque, Croydon, CR0 4TD

A CIP catalogue record for this book is available from the British Library

ISBN   978 1 85459 573 7